First Class Answers in History

Edited by Ralph Bennett

First Class Answers in History

Weidenfeld and Nicolson, London

ISBN 0 297 76687 2

Weidenfeld and Nicolson
11 *St John's Hill, London SW*11

Printed in Great Britain by
Willmer Brothers Limited, Birkenhead

Contents

Introduction

Ralph Bennett

To propose to set down the difference between a good answer in a history examination and an outstanding one may seem a rash undertaking. Surely, it will be urged, there is not one single way of excelling, but a multitude so large as to baffle description? Is it also implied that the line which separates the good from the better is the same as that which divides the First Class from the rest when the results are published? If so, the enterprise must appear still more imprudent.

All this has been prominently in the minds of the contributors to this book. We were all at first a little sceptical when it was suggested that we should write it, yet we all felt a strong pull towards the undertaking. We could not go about our business of teaching and examining if we could not tell good essays from bad ones. Part of the difference at least must in any case be quite easy to detect, for every individual who reads seriously is accustomed to distinguish excellence from mediocrity when he attaches more weight to one piece of evidence than another or accepts this argument rather than that – an obvious reflection indeed, but one which underlies an important point made in several of the chapters which follow: the difference between the scholar's book and the candidate's answer is, in history at any rate, almost entirely one of degree and hardly at all one of kind, for both are products of the same type of thought and both are judged in the same way. A distinction so familiar and in such regular use can surely be isolated and studied. To describe it as exactly as possible might benefit some of the regrettably large company of those who fail to do themselves justice in examinations – a welcome prospect, for the professional teacher suffers real distress when his pupils do not secure results worthy of their abilities in the examinations for which he has helped them to prepare.[1]

This book sets out to offer practical advice,[2] then, not a philosophy of history or some new approach. Moreover, this advice is directed mainly towards the top stratum of the class-list; many more are sincerely spoken of in June as having 'a good chance of a First' than are seen in July to have achieved it, and it is them that we aim principally to help.[3] But if we purvey no grandiose new philosophy of history, neither do we peddle a gimmick so novel and complex that only the cleverest can use it. Excellence in historical writing consists of simple and solid virtues, not of facile tricks and gaudy gadgets. It can therefore be appreciated by all who have the wit and the diligence to seek it; it is no monopoly of those who possses superior talents. This explains a deliberate ambiguity in the title of this book. We claim to distinguish first-class quality from the second-rate with some certainty; but we do not pretend to tell anyone 'How to Get a First', nor do we guarantee that a First will be the sure reward of following our advice.

There are at least three good reasons for this. History is never complete, and there can never be total agreement among historians except about simple issues; like witnesses of a street accident, they see the same thing from different angles. It would therefore be absurd to suppose either that a candidate could write down the whole truth about anything in forty-five minutes or that anyone could tell him how to do so. It follows from this same incompleteness that to examine in history is to use one's experience and discrimination to record the *impression* that this answer or this candidate is better than that, the one showing penetration, insight and originality[4] while the other presents no more than a competent *rechauffé* of second-hand ideas. Of course the impressionistic element in marking is rigorously controlled through careful scrutiny of the evidence cited or overlooked by the candidate and by close attention to his ability to argue a case with logic and prudence; but the nature of historical study itself determines that at the crucial moments of an examiners' meeting decisions turn upon one man's *impression* that a particular answer deserves alpha and another's that it is worth no more than beta. But since an impression is not a totally rational thing, susceptible of proof or disproof after the fashion of a theorem in Euclidean geometry, there can be no precise definition of it and no exact guide to ways of creating any particular impression in another's mind. Lastly, it is presumably because of all this that fewer Firsts are usually given in history examinations than in most other subjects; and if the line is drawn so severely there is bound to be disagreement over where to place it.

A first-class candidate will not necessarily get a First, therefore, and even the best advice cannot positively guarantee success. But there is nevertheless a very great measure of agreement about the qualities which make for excellence, and it is these which the following pages attempt to describe and illustrate. The remarkable similarity of views expressed by seven writers upon very widely different aspects of historical study proceeds from a spontaneous convergence of opinion, not from any imposed editorial norm, and is in itself probably our best proof that first-class qualities can be identified and described. But our joint teaching and examining experience may seem more immediately convincing evidence; our credentials should be presented before I try to summarize our conclusions.

When we wrote these chapters, we were six university lecturers and one assistant university lecturer at Cambridge; Dr Pullan took office as professor at Manchester in January 1973. In varying combinations we have examined with each other in the Historical Tripos so often that we are familiar with each other's standards and know that we can draw up a class-list without major conflict of opinion. We all examine candidates for admission to our colleges each year, and two of us have considerable experience of A-level examining. We regularly supervise men and women reading for the Historical Tripos. We can thus all claim to be well acquainted with examination candidates' problems from several external points of view; in addition, all but myself took a first degree less than fifteen years ago, and still retain fairly vivid memories of what it is like to be under examination pressure. Only two of us have much first-hand experience of conditions in universities other than Oxford and Cambridge, but there are so many reasons to think that standards of excellence are not defined differently elsewhere that this cannot in itself detract much from the value of our opinions.

Few of those who read this book are likely to sit examinations in all the subjects it covers. The remainder would do well not to pass over the chapters which do not directly concern them, however. By a fortunate chance, each contributor has approached his task in a different way, so that they complement one another; and all make points which are valid outside the bounds of the particular subject. Thus Mr Brogan's advice – prevent your friends from fussing you, eat a good breakfast, and go into the examination room with a mind uncluttered with excessive detail so that you can think clearly[5] – does not apply only to those reading American history, and any of Dr Hyam's four types of essay[6] can be written in other subjects as well as the expansion of Europe. Mrs Bowker uses examples from the twelfth, sixteenth and seventeenth centuries to demonstrate how best to overcome the problems of exposition, but modern historians could learn much (though they would apply it to different cases) from her warning against crudely distinguishing Church from state when both classifications in fact cover the same men, or from the psychological explanation of events as illustrated by the marriage projects of Queen Elizabeth I.[7] Again, Mr Trebilcock shows how large masses of rather recalcitrant evidence may best be handled, but (as he himself points out) the technique can be used with only relatively slight modification in other fields besides nineteenth-century English economic history.[8]

By direct statement or clear implication, the question of pattern-making by historians is touched on several times in the following pages. 'We cannot hold together huge masses of particulars without putting them into some kind of structure'[9] is a view which makes special appeal to the examination candidate, who needs a framework upon which to hang ideas and information ready for instant recall; yet patterns can easily become dangerously abstract and unreal, as Dr Pullan shows.[10] The test of a pattern is its credibility,[11] but credibility too has its criteria. Several recommendations are made here for retaining the pattern but avoiding the attendant dangers. Among them is the cultivation of a sense of time as an insurance against crediting the men of the past with opinions which had not been heard of when they were alive or blaming them for mistakes which they had the means neither to foresee nor to avoid; this should make them more likely to emerge as living realities and not as stiff-jointed mechanical artifacts in whose plastic veins blood never flowed. The abstract pattern is too often constructed out of words ending with 'ism';[12] because these are so amorphous they easily become jargon and tend to falsify history instead of casting it into a convenient and credible mould. Lastly, the pattern is only a model or working hypothesis to be continually modified and never regarded as fixed or sacrosanct.

The candidate's chief protection against these dangers is his common sense, a commodity which is freely available but too seldom used. Its value is manifested in widely differing ways. At one extreme lies the oldest advice of all – 'Answer the question'. This is still the best single warning to keep in mind; let common sense tell you that 'This is not an answer to the question set' must condemn even the finest essay, for the good reason that it is hard to credit irrelevance (whether accidental or apparently deliberate) with intellectual distinction. At the opposite extreme, common sense may suggest the direct approach, the simple and revealing line of thought that may have escaped all those who have dealt with a particular issue previously; it pulls the rug from under the feet of pretentiousness and opens the door to independence of mind and to that form of originality of which the best examination answers are truly capable. An examiner does not expect to derive new factual information from a candidate's answer, but he may occasionally admit with real sincerity 'I have learned something from this script'. Even in economic history, where statistics reign, new insights are possible even to the innumerate, who cannot overload himself with figures in the examination-room but is as capable as the more mathematically-minded of grasping their main significance in the course of his preparation.[13]

The amateur can still occasionally beat the professional at the game of history, for history is a game that any intelligent person can play if he is prepared to discipline himself. The professional is someone who over a long period has voluntarily imposed on himself the discipline which is necessary to distinguish evidence suitable for the purpose in hand from that which is unsuitable, and has thereby fitted himself to deal fairly with the complexities of the past. But the amateur – respecting the discipline as much, although he has submitted himself to it for a shorter time – may, if he keeps his head, see much farther than he expects. He can then be tolerably certain to reap his due reward; for the act of keeping his head has set him apart from the crowd and ranked him with the relatively few who neither cloak the issue before them in a tangle of impressive but meaningless jargon words, nor by misplaced subtlety fragment the truth into particles which cannot recompose into a credible image of the past.

The road which leads to better answers is broad and quite well paved. Contrary to common belief, there are no traps concealed beneath its surface; the traveller may begin his journey along it with confidence and a quiet mind. 'Fool', cried Harry Smith when his armour turned aside the Highlander's trick dagger-blow at the beginning of the great fight between the Clan Chattan and the Clan Quhele which forms the climax of Scott's *Fair Maid of Perth*, 'Fool, you were taught the thrust but not the parry.' We are guilty of no such deception. What we have written here is sincere belief and the fruit of experience; nothing has been added for effect, and nothing held back to preserve the secrets of a craft. If it seems plain and straightforward, that is perhaps because the truth is seldom as complicated as it looks. Just as there are no deliberately 'catch questions' in examination papers, but what is asked in them has to be understood in its plain meaning and thoroughly scrutinized, not in search of snares but in order to extract the maximum advantage from every opportunity it offers, so there is no hidden mystery about good history writing.

The light that illuminates the road towards it most brightly is the light of true enjoyment. 'If history is not fun,' writes Dr Steinberg, 'it is not for you. Find yourself another subject.'[14] He is right, where Catherine Morland in *Northanger Abbey* was wrong: 'History, real solemn history, I cannot be interested in . . . I read a little of it as a duty, but it tells me nothing that does not vex or weary me.' If history is solemn, and you read it as a duty, then you are in for trouble. But if you enjoy it you may find the barrier which separates the First Class from the rest a great deal more fragile than you expected.

Notes

1. For the purpose of this book, the system of written examinations is taken for granted and no opinion is expressed about its merits or demerits. However, a statement of what seven experienced examiners hold to be excellence in history writing may assuage some of the fears of those who feel disadvantaged by the system and may enlighten its opponents about the way in which it works in practice. The following chapters should at least show that the 'victims' have less to fear than some of them believe and that the 'judge-cum-executioner' sets out to give fair sentence by known standards and is arbitrary only in the sense that he has a duty to arrange the candidates in various classes.
2. But it confines itself to advice bearing directly upon the writing of examination answers, and deliberately refrains from dealing with a number of matters where personal contact and discussion are vital. We do not presume to usurp the functions of a tutor or director of studies, whose advice is indispensable over matters (the established conventions of a particular syllabus, for example) where proper guidance depends on familiarity with local circumstances, and without whose knowledge of a candidate's personality and temperament a responsible answer cannot be given to important questions like the number of hours a day to work, the best choice between alternative papers, the relation of style to content, and so forth.
3. We have had undergraduates mainly in mind throughout, but it follows from what has been said in the previous paragraph that our suggestions should also be useful to candidates for A-level and university entrance.
4. The use of this word does not imply that an examination candidate can make a research worker's contribution to positively new knowledge, of course. But it is in common use to denote the liveliness and independence of mind shown by the best candidates, which in some cases can approach very closely to originality in the strict sense; cf. below, p. 5.
5. Below, p. 121.
6. Below, p. 138.
7. Below, pp. 69, 78–81.
8. Below, pp. 88, 105.
9. C. S. Lewis, *They Asked for a Paper*, p. 11.
10. Below, p. 41.

11. Below, p. 103.
12. Below, pp. 36, 57, 148–9.
13. Below, 91.
14. Below, p. 62.

as king (their ancestors had already turned down one proposal to dethrone the sacred descendants of Clovis) if recent experience had not gradually convinced them that in anointing the new royal family and thereby approving the constitutional revolution Boniface and the pope were giving it the blessing of Heaven. The medieval centuries are full of this divine right of kings. It was still believed to work wonders in 1484, when the French States-General, which had been convened to deal with the succession, urged the immediate coronation of a new king as a means of avoiding military disasters like Agincourt, remarking of Joan of Arc's Charles VII 'sitost qu'il fut couronné, ne cessa de prospérer et de avoir victoire sur ses ennemis'.[6]

The kings who claimed divine right were almost bound to protect the religion from which it was derived even if they had no particularly strong personal faith. At the end of the Dark Ages many of them found that they could more readily win ascendancy over their subjects if they assumed sponsorship of the 'peace movement' through which some of the clergy were seeking to give practical effect to everyone's desire for security by emphasizing Christianity's message of peace on earth – that is to say, the kings began to pose as the only authorized guardians of the primary social need for law and order. By the middle of the twelfth century – in the legislation of Frederick Barbarossa, Henry II and Louis VII, for example – this bit of semi-enlightened power-politics had become a central feature of royal activity and had acquired legal and theological theories to back it, and a start had been made with the establishment of courts (and even a primitive police system) to enforce the royal monopoly. While on the one hand this entitled and enabled kings to take firm action to suppress disturbers of the peace, on the other it forced them to justify their actions by some criterion higher than mere expediency and less subjective than their own unfettered will. Thus something which began as a way of extending the royal power became later on a means of restricting it; and when, as in Magna Carta, this happened, the final upshot was that church, king and society were more closely knit than ever and all three probably stronger into the bargain.

To understand that the institutional Church never really

wanted to dispense with lay influence (indeed, at first positively welcomed it) but simply to moderate the severity of kingly rule, to recognize that the state could never be truly secular because it needed the Church's wealth, propaganda and manpower to run its own affairs, to realize that (at any rate until towards the end of the Middle Ages) the descriptions 'Church' and 'state' often covered pretty well the same men[7] – to do this is to discover how one important part of medieval society actually worked. The discovery gives protection against the surprisingly common error of seeing a modern-style conflict between two opposed and mutually exclusive systems. A 'typically medieval' principle is thereby revealed, and with it a simple and effective way of writing better medieval history.

Since I have just used the words 'Church' and 'state',[8] this must be the place for an immediate warning against the habit of using abstract concepts instead of concrete examples – a habit which has become distressingly common lately, for the growing popularity of ecclesiastical theory has been accompanied by a tendency to isolate it from the events which gave it rise. 'Outline' syllabuses covering ten or a dozen centuries are common, and the natural consequence is that the European Middle Ages are not studied in detail or with the intensity accorded to English history. It will not do, however, to skate gaily over any thin patches of ice which may result by using vague, abstract or jargon terms, for these hardly ever mean anything worth saying. It was a missionary bishop and an aspirant to the throne who allied with such tremendous results in the middle of the eighth century, not two general tendencies. No doubt what they did 'marked a new stage in the relations of Church and state' (or some such tired historical cliché), but this is not by any means the best way of describing their attitude towards each other. It is even more tempting for the medievalist to de-nature his characters and take cowardly refuge in lifeless abstractions than it is for the modern historian, for the simple reason that it seems more difficult to penetrate the motives and understand the action of eighth- than of eighteenth-century people. But it is even more dangerous, because – for exactly the same reason – the medievalist's abstractions have still less chance of being anything like the originals they are supposed to represent. To offer them is to open up a credibility gap between writer and reader, and the result is much the same whether you are reading the professor's book or he is reading your examination answer: both readers can tell pretty quickly whether the writers have managed to discuss the real actions of real people or not, for cardboard dummies are as dull to read about as they are hard to believe in. *You* will probably throw his book aside as boring; *he* will give your answer a very ordinary mark (not, probably, a rank bad one, if it is tolerably well-informed – for unless examiners are charitable they fail too many candidates). You may have cited a fair selection of evidence and arrived at some acceptable conclusions, but many others will have done the same and you have not excelled them by showing that you realize that history is about people who were once as alive as you are.

This has to be borne in mind when writing about any period, but it applies with particular force to the Middle Ages. When we think of a state, we think of a central government. At a time when feudal privilege, ecclesiastical immunity and economic localism were the rule, however, most of the governing that got done at all was done by local authorities of one kind or another. From very small beginnings indeed, there slowly developed at the centre a will and a power to curb these local authorities. Because the development is interesting in itself, and because it had a great importance later on, we study it closely, noting how new courts and new kinds of officials appear, for instance. Hence it becomes easy to forget both how very gradual the development was and how much it depended on the person of the king. There was very little government at all; but the king *was* the government in every century before the thirteenth, and his personal influence was paramount long afterwards. So long as the court was constantly on the move and waggon-transport restricted the number of records the early civil servants could carry about, so long as domestic and foreign politics could depend on face-to-face confrontations (Barbarossa and Henry the Lion at Chiavenna in 1176, for instance, or – more tragically – the dauphin Charles and duke John of Burgundy on the bridge of Montéreau in 1419) an individual ruler's personality, motives and intentions – even his momentary impulses[9] – were vitally important because they might decide action.

All the same, it is far from easy to avoid writing in abstract terms about 'imperial policy', 'papal designs' or the like, even while realizing that their exact nature (and perhaps their very existence) may be in doubt because the right kind of evidence is lacking.[10] Even in the case of Boniface and Pippin, where Boniface's letters make it more plentiful than is common in the earlier centuries, some of our conclusions rest on probable inference not direct knowledge. If Leo III and Gregory VII had left memoirs, there would have been less need to speculate why one pope crowned Charlemagne and the other forgave Henry IV, and many books would have remained unwritten. It is hard enough to understand that although he restricted the scope of their activity Louis IX did not envisage that royal justice should take over the business of the ecclesiastical and baronial courts, but it is probably easier to do so than to define royal 'policy' in the light of the understanding. The sources for medieval history are nothing like so scanty as some answers to questions in outline papers rashly suggest, but most of them are much more informative about the 'what' than the 'why' of the events they relate; yet explanation is more instructive than a mere chronicle, however intricate the narrative and however important its testimony, for it is the only key we have to an understanding of the past (incidentally it also makes a pattern which is far easier to remember in the examination room). It may not matter much in the end that we have to consider the expedients by which King George of Bohemia sought about 1460 to retain the loyalty of subjects divided between two religions although we know little positive about his own beliefs; but judgements of Louis XI's bizarre first actions as king would be better founded if it were possible to determine exactly what he expected to gain by his sudden and unconditional revocation of the Pragmatic Sanction on 22 November 1461.[11] Conversely, because Nicholas V had already signified the papacy's acceptance of the Renaissance by founding the Vatican library, it would be easy to suppose the famous humanist Aeneas Sylvius Piccolomini a natural choice for the tiara in 1458 did we not possess, in Aeneas's own *Commentaries,*[12] a racy (and very 'slanted') account of the political in-fighting among the cardinals during the night of 18–19 August which ended in the discomfiture of the hotly-fancied French candidate and the triumph of an Italian; the fact that this is the oldest extant inside story of a papal election is a useful caution against jumping to even apparently obvious conclusions about earlier elections where the motives of the participants are less well known.

Historians often fabricate policies gratuitously. Twelfth-century French and German history offer prime examples of the temptation to construct them out of nothing and to ascribe motives where none may have existed.

One reason for the success of the Capetian royal house was that for nearly 250 years the king's eldest son was always old enough to be associated in the kingship before his father died, so that the succession was uncontested. By the end of the 250 years, the French crown had risen from insignificance to something like mastery of the realm. Was this the operation of cause and effect? Examination answers often rest far more weight of deduction on the evidence than it can possibly bear, although the most-used book on the Capetians issues an express warning against doing so.[13] His unchallenged succession proves nothing about each king's thoughts and purposes, still less does it suggest that each in turn maintained a consistent and deliberate policy inherited from his predecessor. There is no positive evidence of such a thing, and every probability is against it:[14] political and military conditions alone changed so much between the late tenth and the mid-thirteenth century that it is in the highest degree unlikely that Hugh Capet or Robert II could have formulated such a 'policy' in terms which would still have been comprehensible in St Louis' time, or even (to dilute the idea somewhat) that they could have conceived it sensible or profitable to try, so little did their own fragile standing warrant illusions of future grandeur. Why, then, fly in the face of these obvious truths and imply the opposite?

An elaborate explanation which rests on doubtful premisses should always be rejected if a simpler solution can be found. It took the first five Capetians all their time to prevent the crown's rights from being entirely swamped by their vassals', and the next (Louis VII) made a political blunder big enough to have wrecked the monarchy's chances for ever.[15] Is it not therefore largely hindsight which prompts so many to write as if there were something about the situation to which Philip Augustus succeeded in 1180 which made his triumph certain? If to begin with you examine his actions one by one, obliterating the end of the story from your mind until you reach it, you may understand a little more of the motives behind them, and may conclude that luck played as large a part as the king's political skill in bringing about the final result, and a far larger part than all the allegedly predisposing circumstances. I think I dislike 'Account for the successes of Philip Augustus' more than any question I have ever seen in a medieval history paper, because it so obviously suggests that there were deep and powerful causes at work which a properly prepared candidate should be able to list in order, assessing the contribution of each and showing that the total adds up to a neat one hundred per cent.

By an even more extravagant distillation of theory from imprudently selected fact, candidates often fix their eyes so firmly on the non-feudal institutions which the French monarchy had at its disposal by the end of the thirteenth century that they are compelled to regard Louis IX as a saintly aberration from the Machiavellian norm of the Capetian house, and to conclude that Philip IV's reign marks the culmination of two centuries of deliberate endeavour because he was victoriously 'anti-feudal' and because he exposed the hollowness of the papacy's claims to universal rule. This travesty of the truth is encouraged by the common custom of cutting short the medieval syllabus about 1300. The recrudescence of feudal and aristocratic separatism (France's main handicap during the Hundred Years War) is consequently overlooked and the fourteenth-century anti-climax prevented from playing its proper role of demonstrating that the 'victory' of Philip IV was in some respects a sham. This has the further consequence of obscuring the fancifulness of the idea that a medieval king could be 'anti-feudal' (it is as fanciful as it would be to suppose that a government could be 'anti-industrial' today, because it is erected upon the negation of the strongest force in contemporary society). Similarly, only ignorance of the way in which kings and popes got on together behind the scenes during the Avignon period and later can permit the Anagni episode to be presented as the crushing victory of a new 'national' monarchy over an antiquated international papacy. No doubt great changes came over Europe between 1300 and 1350, but it can be nearly fatal to use them as a reason for severing the 'Later Middle Ages' too sharply from the 'High Middle Ages': generalizations about either will be even more inaccurate if they are made without regard to the other.

However, it would not be fair to deny that large and (to modern eyes) somewhat inscrutable forces did play a part in medieval events, or to pretend that it is always easy to avoid abstractions. 'Feudalism' is one which is used far too freely. It had a lot to do with Capetian success, but to explain the success solely in terms of feudalism is to argue in a small and very vicious circle. The term was not invented until after the end of the Middle Ages, and it serves to describe a whole social system and a tangle of relationships which naturally changed a good deal during the five or so centuries of their greatest influence. Is so huge and amorphous a concept likely to be the sharp and delicate instrument which is needed to dissect the events of a single reign and explain them? Particularly if (as Marc Bloch said) the nobles' proclivity to violence was the hallmark of feudalism[16] – that is to say, that the centrifugal outweighed the centripetal tendency within it?

All discussions of feudalism turn at last into debates about these two tendencies. A good way of demonstrating that feudalism did not 'inevitably' or 'by its very nature' tend in *either* direction is to compare France and Germany in the wide terms of a Tripos question I set a few years ago: 'What can be learned about the government and social structure of the Empire and France in the late twelfth and early thirteenth centuries from a comparison between Henry the Lion's loss of Saxony and Bavaria in 1180 and King John's loss of Normandy in 1202?' It is a fascinating and instructive exercise, and one which is attempted surprisingly seldom. Begin by listing some of the things which are common to both cases: an energetic king; a feudal link between king and great nobles (newer and less complete in Germany than in France, of course); a personally recalcitrant and politically almost independent great vassal; a decision against the great vassal by the royal court (composed of his equals in status) which was unimpeachably 'correct' in feudal law; the decision of the court executed by force of royal arms. The feudal nature of society (the French and German varieties of which were at that very moment approximating more closely to each other than before) was thus intimately concerned at every stage of both affairs and evidently shaped the political outcome, the fall of both recalcitrants. How strange, then – if feudalism was the decisive influence – that the long-term constitutional results were the exact opposites of each other! Now let the strangeness make you pause for a moment's reflection. The eventual outcome was indeed very different in both countries. But how soon was this certain, and was it the direct and exclusive consequence of the two famous cases? Did it not rather derive from something older than feudalism and largely outside it? If you ask why the French nobles did not prevent their king from annexing Normandy, making a valuable addition to his demesne, and thereby from setting the monarchy firmly on the road to success (remember not to draw this conclusion too easily: Philip Augustus prudently waited ten years, until Bouvines, before doing so), you will get a new insight into crown – vassal relationships at the end of the twelfth century, and you will begin to realize how politically inert feudalism really was 'by its nature'. To ask why the German nobles did the opposite is to confirm what you know already about the traditional hostility between them and the crown. But inquire instead whether *Leihezwang* was a law which had to be observed henceforth or a precedent which might not be followed (how often did Henry VI and Frederick II disregard it, and with what object?), why Frederick Barbarossa was so secure and so imposing a figure in the ten years (1180–90) after Gelnhausen, and (above all) whether, had the monarchy's fortunes not so soon been shattered by two decades of civil war, we should not all now probably be regarding the *Leihezwang* of 1180 as a final flicker of Dark Age ducal autonomy rather than the last straw which broke the monarchy's back and kept it paralysed until 1871 – a bout of self-questioning like this will lead to so much better an understanding of the relationship between feudalism and government that subsequent essays are bound to reflect it. And there will probably be two far from insignificant 'spin-offs' as well: more hesitation before letting the deadly word 'inevitable' creep into your vocabulary, and a greater readiness to give Frederick II the credit which he deserves but is so often denied.[17]

The policy manufacturers have a happy time with Frederick Barbarossa. They can be exposed by similar methods and with equally beneficial results. Barbarossa spent so many years fighting the Italians that it has to be presumed that he did so deliberately. He has often been credited with a sort of appeasement plan in Germany as well, and since the grants to Henry the Lion and the establishment of the duchy of Austria (which form the evidence for it) date from just before the 1158 Roncaglia decrees, it looks as if his immediate object was to ensure peace in his rear while he fought on the Italian front (are we obliged to go further and imagine that he also had the more distant goal of turning on Germany and cleaning it up as soon as he had conquered Italy?). A third element has been added lately: the intention to create a kind of Alpine redoubt to serve as a base from which to launch Italian offensives. There emerges a logically-constructed plan, its interlocking parts well calculated to cope with matters as diverse as the pride and ambition of German nobles, urban taxation in Lombardy, the spiritual threats and political adroitness of popes, the danger of a war on two fronts and the crucial issue of timing. Natural scepticism may enable you to see through Munz's persuasive sales-talk for his 'Grand Design' to the flimsiness of the real evidence for it,[18] but since almost everyone assumes some sort of plan you may never think of asking the vital first question of all: What proof is there that Barbarossa conceived his Italian and German actions as mutually-supporting parts of a single deliberately-planned whole? If so, it will be a shock to discover that there is almost none at all. Afterwards, however, it may be much easier to appreciate that Barbarossa may have had quite different motives – such as an imprecise but strongly-felt, conservative notion of ensuring that good order was kept and proper justice done throughout his dominions – and to realize that the chief thing wrong with the whole idea of a grandiose plan is the very completeness which makes it so attractive at first sight. It is far too rational for a twelfth-century emperor. It does not fit in at all well with what we know of Barbarossa's temperament and upbringing, for instance, nor with the irrationality of using the first really tranquil years since his coronation to rush off on a crusade when over sixty years of age; for the odds were against his coming back alive and he had not been able to do much to guarantee that his death would not lead to the fifth disputed succession of the century.

'Do not rationalize what may never have been rational in the first place' is a useful antidote against the itch to fabricate policies needlessly. We take the idea of the state and its continuity for granted, like to suppose it acts rationally, and expect statesmen to think several moves ahead like chess players; but things were different in Barbarossa's simpler age (medieval Europe had only just had its first lessons in logical thought from Abelard in philosophy and theology and from the Bolognese in Roman law), when the personality and even the whims of a ruler might determine his actions to a far greater extent. The more complex a pattern we make, the farther we probably depart from reality; Barbarossa may even have had no 'policy' in this sense at all, and the true pattern may be no more than a set of tolerably self-consistent reactions to events as they occurred.[19]

However carefully it is formulated, almost any question on Church history between the Investiture Contest and the Reformation will unhappily lead some candidates into the limbo of the second-rate because (moved, it seems, by anachronistic echoes of an Anglican Protestant fury they probably manifest in no other aspect of their lives) they insist on using the windy and ambiguous words 'reform' and 'abuse' (or 'corruption') like flails to belabour an institution they have not tried hard enough to understand. Few stop to reflect that the actions they label 'corrupt' were usually no more than the inevitable (the word is justified for once!) consequences of that curious mixture of aspiration and worldliness which can be seen in the collaboration of Boniface and Pippin. It is scarcely possible to avoid the words altogether, but it is best to approach them with as much caution as a booby-trap. To paraphrase them for a moment by 'right' and 'wrong' will at least show up their essentially subjective values. Alternatively, think of 'reform' as being used then in the same way that 'democracy' is often used today – as the magic word without which the propaganda for any political system is incomplete, even though the systems so labelled often diverge widely from each other. It is largely because 'reform' and 'abuse' were intended by their medieval users to have an emotive effect that they have to be treated so carefully today.

Another way of escaping danger might be to list all the various shades of meaning encountered during a course of reading. How different was the sense Hildebrand gave to 'reform' from what it meant to the Cluniac monks from whom he took it over? – and why?[20] If he gave it a more political twist than they, does this make him any less of a 'reformer' in the conditions of his time? Ask the same conundrum a hundred and fifty years later, and force yourself to write down precisely why you think Innocent III's actions show him to have been more concerned with politics than with pure religion (a look at the legislation he promoted at the Fourth Lateran Council of 1215 will induce a proper caution) and why it is right to assert, as so many answers unfortunately do, that he was a 'political pope' (what does the phrase actually mean, by the way?) of the worst kind who set the papacy's course in the wrong direction. This is no easy task if you play fair with the evidence and don't read history backwards, but it ought to result in a better appreciation of the immense power Innocent wielded, the life-and-death problems he faced and the hair-raising decisions he had to take. Here, too, is a chance to correct another mistake which is encouraged by the use of large, vague and emotive terms – the mistake of giving a whole segment of history a uniform character ('an age of reform', 'a period of decline', and the like), thus making it static and obliterating not only its life and movement but also even the very actions which gave it that character. The eighteen years of Innocent's pontificate were punctuated by tremendous emergencies – some desperate and threatening, some temptingly beckoning him into vast new fields of papal influence – and it is upon the action he took to meet each in turn that an estimate of him depends. Another possibility is to go back a little in time and look at the same issue at the moment when it first became really hot: read St Bernard *On Consideration*[21] and note how delicately and how realistically he shows that the spirit of reform can temper – but not restrict – the papal power he not only accepts but triumphantly fortifies; this alone is enough to stop you using the battle-axe of 'reform' to cut off the head of every medieval prelate who was not completely passive when confronting evils he had the power to prevent. Read two recent books – Peter Partner's *Lands of St Peter* and Walter Ullmann's *Short History of the Papacy in the Middle Ages*[22] – and discover from one why the popes had to have territory and defend it and from the other why they felt that their claims to omnipotence were sound; having done so, you will very likely still want to criticize them for doing too little for 'reform', but your criticism will be less raucous because it will be based on a truer perception of their difficulties and responsibilities, and what you write will correspond a little more closely to what actually made them behave as they did.

Next, carry the operation a stage further by asking just how it came about that, as Boniface VIII said, recent experience as well as ancient history showed that laymen hated clerics, and see whether the blame for this can fairly be laid at anyone's door. Alternatively, reconstruct the intricate disputes which ended with John XXII condemning as heretics all those who taught the poverty of Christ, and then reappraise St Francis and the healing powers of 'reform' when carried to New Testament extremes.[23] Finally, try to determine why 'reform' meant something to do with Church *government* by the time the Council of Constance burned John Hus, and by studying the history of Gallicanism (another emotive word with many shades of meaning) note how on the eve of the Reformation some of the keenest 'reformers' were not clergy at all.[24] Inexact, windy and unhistorical generalizations will scarcely survive treatment like this. Essays written after it will be of a higher quality – and they are more likely to be answers to the question actually asked and not to that different and far less interesting question which candidates so often insist on answering.

Most of the illustrations used so far depend for their full effect on chronology. A delicate feeling for the passage of time is a primary requisite for a medieval historian, but this is as hard to acquire as it is to distinguish the relative ranges of two targets when both are a long distance away. If you know anything of arms and armour, castle and cathedral building, or handwriting and illumination, one of them may serve as a range-finder. At all events, seek by one means or another to become sensitive to intervals as short as half a century. This is difficult until one's own experience has become long enough to detect differences between remembered decades, but not impossible. I remember first learning the trick by reflecting upon the changes my grandfather had seen during his lifetime: he was born in the year of the Great Exhibition, remained so much a man of the railway age that he always called a motor-car's radiator its boiler, and died as Hitler came to power and television was invented. Almost any example will serve to train one's sense of time – simply take any two years half a century or so apart and try to relive the experiences of some prominent man born in one and dying in the other; unexpected shafts of light will soon begin to illuminate what was until now the flat backdrop of the past, and valuable perspectives will appear. The 'age of St Bernard' is one of the most instructive examples. A little beyond both ends of it, Legnano (1176) is clearly worlds away from Canossa (1077) – but does not the Council of Pavia (1160) seem almost as far from the *Pravilegium* of 1111 although they are only fifty years apart? How much has this to do with the Twelfth Century Renaissance, and with what aspects of it in particular? Was it at this time, or later, that the towns first made their mark on the European scene? (Where did they do this, by the way? Was it in the end a surprisingly *small* mark? This last may prevent you from mindlessly trundling out the juggernaut 'rise of the towns' when you can't think of a real explanation for something or other.) Was St Bernard the first statesman to reckon with religious as well as communal disaffection, and how and where were the two connected?[25] How different was St Bernard's (1090–1153) experience of religion and politics from that of Pope Alexander III (c. 1110–81), St Francis's (1181–1226) from St Bonaventura's (1221–74)?

Since all this is little more than a useful trick of thought, it calls for no knowledge beyond the ordinary run. Suitable stimuli can be provided by things as various as a time-chart with parallel columns for information of different kinds and books like Sir Kenneth Clark's *Civilisation* (1969) (where the divisions of time, as well as some of the judgements, are instructive to the mainly political historian precisely because they are not always the same as his own) or Iris Origo's *Merchant of Prato* (1957), which shows how one individual coped with the tension between piety and profit-making in the early fifteenth century. Moreover, even to read the time-chart across horizontally will engender a profitable compulsion to remember what was contemporary with what and (as in the example of feudalism and the constitution, 1180 and 1202) to refrain from putting things into unhistorically separate water-tight compartments and keeping them there just because this makes for convenient revision.

After a sense of time, a sense of place. Whether they realize it or not, most people stand in imagination at some geographical point or other when contemplating a train of past events, or mentally locate a king or pope at some particular spot. The habit has drawbacks as well as advantages. The natural instinct to look across into Europe from the English side of the Channel may misleadingly make the effective extension of papal authority to England in the late twelfth century seem like the invasion of something suited to the continent but alien here, for instance. On the other hand, since the intellectual and diplomatic capital of medieval Europe was usually either Rome or Paris, to observe events in imagination from one or the other will help to put them into proper perspective. But since the emperor, and not the king of France, was the dominant European ruler for most of the period 1050–1250, why not a German town instead of Paris? The schools of Mont Ste Geneviève are part of the answer, of course, but an essential difference between the two countries is thrown into relief simply by remembering that the Saxon and Salian emperors lacked a capital because their subjects' restiveness made constant journeying the best means of enforcing royal authority, while the weaker Capetians were constrained by the same pressures to live mainly in Paris, where later on they drew rich dividends from what had been a compulsory investment. The eleventh-century French and German royal itineraries printed in the *Grosser Historischer Weltateas*[26] illustrate a little of this; much more can be learned from the maps which accompany Carlrichard Brühl's study of the emperors' fiscal rights[27] – notably from one which corrects the habit of regarding Frederick II as an Italian interested only in the south by showing how often he visited certain German towns. The well-known calculation that the popes spent 122 years out of Rome and only 82 in it between 1100 and 1304[28] checks a natural tendency to think of them as fixed there by indicating the precarious nature of their hold on the city; and by also preventing the Avignon Captivity from seeming more novel than it really was, these simple figures help to drive home the lesson that, after two centuries of growing administrative sophistication and the usually victorious assertion of power, the traditions of the see of Peter had become so small a part of the foundation of papal authority that they could be dispensed with, for now *ubi papa ibi Roma.*

But all this is inside Europe. The Byzantinist can look at the continent from outside whenever he chooses; others may find that their conventional judgements receive a stimulating shock if they stand in imagination on the banks of the Oder with the armies of Batu Khan in April 1241 and observe from afar the weakness and divisions of a Europe unprepared militarily or psychologically to resist the threatened Mongol onslaught: an emperor at the end of his patience with a bitter and intransigent pope's refusal to make peace, and about to take revenge for repeated excommunications by an act of piracy and the capture of a score of prelates on their way to a Church council; Italian cities still reeling under the blow of Cortenuova four years before and still disunited, but with their whole attention concentrated on the fight against Frederick II; St Louis, still not quite secure on the throne, apprehensively awaiting the imminent outbreak of the La Marche rebellion and hence not yet the sage and respected leader of Christendom which he had become by the time he launched his crusade in 1248; Henry III of England at constant odds with barons who make repeated but vain efforts to restrain his dictatorial tendencies. The urgency of the 1241 crisis is forgotten because it never developed, but it is salutary to be reminded that there was a darker side to the confident and settled Europe of the Thomist age.

The Mongols devastated Hungary and irretrievably changed the course of Russian history, but they withdrew from the west after only a preliminary skirmish with the Germans.[29] They might have conquered, but could never have held their conquests. Further speculation is unrewarding here, but it can be helpful on other occasions. Perhaps in despair of mastering their intractable materials, economic historians have lately taken to constructing 'counterfactual models' of the nineteenth century; the scepticism with which Mr Trebilcock treats their imaginings[30] need not apply to the less elaborately hypothetical history which can, I think, sometimes help the medieval historian to perceive the full significance of real events by forcing him to reconstruct the next few likely developments as if the outcome of (say) an evenly-matched battle had been different. The familiar example of supposing that Louis XI of France and Charles the Rash of Burgundy had been born to rule each other's realms is still one of the best (the facts that they were quite closely related[31] and that neither much resembled his father in character lends a little verisimilitude to the supposition). Would Charles's rashness have wrecked what looks, under Louis, like the inexorable advance of a kingdom regaining its strength after the Hundred Years War? Would Louis' diplomacy have welded together the scattered and disparate territories of Burgundy and thus added a new state to the map of Europe? The potential consequences for the sixteenth century of an enfeebled France and an established Burgundy are tremendous: driven between France and Germany like a wedge, its base stretching from the Somme to the Zuider Zee and its point touching Basel and Geneva, a stable kingdom of Burgundy might have prevented the destructive wars of Habsburg and Valois; had Holland still become Calvinist, Burgundy might have succeeded (where Bohemia had failed) in reconciling political loyalty with religious division and have given an example of toleration in an age distracted by the murderous conflict of creeds. Some will argue that the dignity of a serious historian should restrain him from such speculation. Even so, he may assuredly ask the questions which prompted it; and if the act of doing this suggests the least ground for supposing that the answers might be 'Yes' then – for him at least – the battle of Nancy on 5 January 1477 will gain new importance as 'a turning-point where history failed to turn' (like the 1848 revolutions) because he will see how easily things could have developed quite differently and therefore how questionable are some favourite cause-and-effect relationships about the recovery of France in the fifteenth century. He will understand the Renaissance state better if this example reminds him that the vainglorious princes of fifteenth-century Europe were constantly assembling conglomerations of territory and as constantly seeing them dissolve again; the political geography of the continent was remarkably fluid, and decisive strength cannot be attributed to 'national' institutions of government at a time when they were still manifestly being exploited for personal or dynastic advantage.

The historian must keep his imagination well under control, but if he does not sometimes give it prudent rein he is like a general who disdains everything his intelligence officers tell him because their information is not all of equally cast-iron reliability. Something more than a complete array of incontrovertible facts (if that were even attainable) is required for the full understanding of the past.

Finally, three pieces of advice which have general application but are particularly relevant to the writing of better answers in medieval history. Since almost all medieval sources were written in Latin, the convenient terms which historians have borrowed from them are sometimes in Latin too. No credit is to be gained from using them rather than their English equivalents, however; and since the standard of Latin in schools has fallen disastrously during the last ten years the attempt to do so may have the opposite result. 'Plenitudo potestas' reveals an ignorance of the third declension genitive but no more knowledge of the thirteenth-century papacy than 'fulness of power'; and I recall finding it very hard to give proper credit to an otherwise very respectable answer which repeated the grammatical monstrosity 'imperium romana' so often that it could not be a slip of the pen but seemed rather to proceed from stupidity. If you want to quote Latin, make sure you quote it correctly, or you may do yourself a disservice.

On the other hand, a quite moderate reading facility in a modern language will give access to books which would otherwise remain out of reach, and will bring advantages commensurate with its surprising rarity. A merely respectable A-level in French is enough, if a little determination be added, to secure acquaintance with stimulating ideas which will be hidden from those who refuse to read any language but English, and an ability to read German will give proportionately greater benefits.

No candidate with any claim to distinction can afford to take his information entirely at second-hand; he must become familiar with sources as well. Language is now no barrier here, for translations of medieval texts have multiplied prodigiously in recent years. There seems to have been no bibliography of them since C. P. Farrar and A. P. Evans: *Bibliography of English Translations from Medieval Sources* (1946), but library catalogues and booksellers' lists will reveal the existence of English versions of many of the authorities cited in the footnotes to standard works. The two best collections of extracts are B. S. Pullan: *Sources for the History of Medieval Europe* (1966) and B. Tierney: *The Crisis of Church and State* (1964); the valuable Nelson (now Oxford) series includes John of Salisbury's *Historia Pontificalis* and a selection of Innocent III's letters; a comparison of E. Emerton: *The Correspondence of Gregory VII* (1932) with T. E. Mommsen and K. F. Morrison: *Imperial Lives and Letters of the Eleventh Century* (1962) makes it possible to follow the stages of the Investiture Contest – these merely by way of example. The variety of translated material available is tremendous, and much of it is in cheap editions. Thorough use of it is one sure way of lending extra quality to essays in medieval history, because it will make them more like what history writing should be and less like examination exercises.

Notes

1. The best alternative to 1453 is probably the scientific revolution of the mid-seventeenth century. It is often put forward, however, as the end of a second medieval 'period' which began between 1300 and 1350; I find it increasingly difficult to believe in the usefulness of this dividing-line, as some of what follows will incidentally show. In his inaugural lecture as Professor of Medieval and Renaissance English at Cambridge in 1954, C. S. Lewis very nearly said that the Middle Ages ended with Jane

Austen; but his real point was the profounder one that the only completely decisive break (industrialization, Darwin, Christianity no longer the accepted norm) between historical periods falls somewhere between her time and our own (*They asked for a Paper* (1962), pp. 9–25). Compare G. Barraclough, *History in a Changing World*, pp. 54–63.

2. St Boniface's letters were translated by C. H. Talbot in *The Anglo-Saxon Missionaries to Germany* (1954). Boniface's career is outlined in S. J. Crawford, *Anglo-Saxon Influence on Western Christendom* (1933, repr. 1966) and by Talbot in *Studies in Church History 6* (1970), pp. 45–8. Different aspects of these events and their causes are discussed in C. Dawson, *The Making of Europe* (1932); W. Levison, *England and the Continent in the Eighth Century* (1946); L. Halphen, *Charlemagne et l'empire carolingien* (1947); D. A. Bullough, *The Age of Charlemagne* (1965); J. M. Wallace-Hadrill, *The Long-Haired Kings* (1962) and *Early Germanic Kingship* (1971); W. Ullmann, *The Carolingian Renaissance and the Idea of Kingship* (1969) and F. L. Ganshof, *The Carolingians and the Frankish Monarchy* (1971).
3. Pirenne's own words were 'Without Mohammed, Charlemagne would have been inconceivable': *Mohammed and Charlemagne* (1935, Eng. tr. 1939), p. 234, but the variant in the text is in common use.
4. Pippin's father Charles Martel took Boniface under his protection in 722 (Talbot, *Missionaries*, p. 75); Boniface recognized how much he owed to this protection when he wrote twenty years later: 'Without the patronage of the Frankish prince I can neither govern the faithful of the Church nor protect the priests, clerics, monks and nuns of God' (Talbot, p. 117).
5. J. Vaesen and J. Charavay: *Lettres de Louis XI* (1883–1909), X, p. 18.
6. A. Bernier: *Journal des Etats-Généraux ... de 1484* (1835), p. 661.
7. Henry II's conflict with Becket can be properly understood only in these terms, for instance: cf. Mrs Bowker's remarks, below, pp. 67, 69.
8. The word 'state' should strictly speaking be avoided, since it cannot be given its modern meaning in a medieval context. I use it for convenience, because suitably qualified paraphrases are long and clumsy; but I write it with a small 's', while using a capital 'C' for 'Church' to signify that the concept *ecclesia* had a very real meaning in the Middle Ages.
9. Or even the state of his digestion? The bad faith of fifteenth-

century kings has been attributed to their extravagantly rich diet and their neglect of fresh vegetables: 'A missing salad and an over-spiced dish may have changed history' (D. B. Wyndham Lewis, *The Soul of Marshal Gilles de Raiz* [1952], p. 37).

10. For some examples, see below pp. 17–18, 21–22.
11. For instance, the latest biography of Louis (P. M. Kendall, *Louis XI* [1971]) has much to say about Louis' behaviour directly after his accession but does not tackle this difficult question.
12. F. A. Gragg and L. C. Gabel, *Memoirs of a Renaissance Pope* (1959) (an abridgement of the *Commentaries*), pp. 79–88.
13. R. Fawtier, *The Capetian kings of France* (1960), p. 227. The essay by B. Smalley in *France: Government and Society*, ed. J. M. Wallace-Handrill, 2nd ed. (1970), pp. 61–82 gives a stimulating short account of the Capetians, while the early chapters of J. R. Shennan, *The Parliament of Paris* (1968) are very informative on one of the main institutions of the monarchy.
14. Including the reaction of a new generation against the views of the old, a consideration easy enough to appreciate today. Well-known medieval examples which had political consequences are Henry (VII) against Frederick II in thirteeenth-century Germany and Louis XI against Charles VII in fifteenth-century France.
15. Or was even public humiliation a small price to pay for release from the daunting task of trying to control and administer so turbulent a province as Aquitaine with the slender resources of men and experience at his disposal? Better, perhaps, let Henry II exhaust himself trying to shoulder the burden? The Capetian king gained in the end, or course, when the Angevins used his court to settle their own disputes; but this could not have been foreseen in 1152.
16. Marc Bloch, *Feudal Society* (1939, Eng. tr. 1961), p. 127 ('To impose on a military caste the renunciation of all private vengeance was neither possible in practice nor conceivable in principle'), pp. 233–6.
17. Barraclough's *Origins of Modern Germany* made facile denigration of Frederick II fashionable. T. C. van Cleve's recent (1972) biography goes some way towards correcting this, though with too little vigour and emphasis where Frederick's attitude towards Germany is concerned.
18. P. Munz, *Frederick Barbarossa* (1969). See pp. 12–19 of the Introduction to my translation of K. Hampe, *Germany under the Salian and Hohenstaufen Emperors* (1973), in which other recent work in medieval German history is also discussed.

19. G. Barraclough, *History in a Changing World* (1955), p. 93.
20. Contrast H. E. J. Cowdrey, *The Cluniacs and the Gregorian Reform* (1970) with G. Tellenbach, *Church, State and Christian Society* (1940).
21. The translation by G. Lewis (1908) is out of print, but a new version is understood to be in preparation.
22. Both published in 1972. R. W. Southern, *Western Society and the Church in the Middle Ages* (1970) is a very valuable general survey.
23. J. R. H. Moorman, *History of the Franciscan Order* (1968) would serve to introduce the more detailed study of M. D. Lambert, *Franciscan Poverty* (1961). No attempt to understand either the spiritual or the institutional aspect of the medieval Church can succeed fully without reference to the writings of Dom David Knowles. In the case of the Franciscans, *Religious Orders in England* (1948), I, pp. 114–253; for St Bernard and the Cistercians, *Monastic Orders in England*, 2nd ed. (1950) pp. 191–266. *From Pachomius to Ignatius* (1966) is as stimulating as it is concise; it discusses all the medieval religious orders.
24. On the whole question of Council and reform, start with H. Jedin, *A History of the Council of Trent* (1949, Eng. tr. 1957), I, pp. 5–165. Some curious examples of secular rulers' interest in reform are in G. G. Coulton, *Five Centuries of Religion* (1950), IV, pp. 120–32, 167, 484–98, etc.
25. This is a difficult and complex question. John of Salisbury's chapter in the *Historia Pontificalis* (ed. Chibnall [1956] pp. 62–5) on Arnold of Brescia in Rome in the 1140s gives an early example of direct connection. R. I. Moore, 'The Origins of medieval heresy', *History*, 183 (1970), pp. 21–36 deals mainly with religious origins. J. L. Nelson, 'Society, theodicy and the origins of heresy', *Studies in Church History*, 9 (1972), pp. 65–79, shows how both the liberty Gregory VII claimed for the Church and the mobility characteristic of a changing social system upset the hierarchical structure of society. These and other relevant themes may be followed in N. Cohn, *The Pursuit of the Millennium* (1957); G. Leff, *Heresy in the Later Middle Ages* (1967); F. Rörig, *The Medieval Town* (1967), J. Le Goff's chapter 'The Town as an Agent of Civilisation', in *Fontana Economic History of Europe*, ed. C. Cipolla (1972), pp. 71–106, D. P. Waley, *The Italian City-Republics* (1969) and J. K. Hyde, *Society and Politics in Medieval Italy* (1973).
26. *Grosser Historischer Weltatlas* (Bayerischer Schulbuch-Verlag, München 1970), II, p. 76. Regular use of maps cannot be too

strongly recommended: it illuminates obscurity and shatters illusions unconsciously held. One look at a map (e.g. *Gr. Hist. Weltatlas*, II, p. 63) will dispel the surprisingly common belief that Charlemagne inherited only France and advanced eastwards along almost the whole Rhine front, because it will show that south Germany had been Frankish (at any rate nominally) since the sixth century. The same kind of misconception often places St Boniface's mission-field much too far west, forgetting that Fulda is a hundred miles north-east of Frankfort, and Ohrdruf still further away in the same general direction.

27. C. Brühl, *Fodrum, Gistum, Servitium Regis* (1968).
28. G. Mollat, *The Popes at Avignon* (1912, Eng. tr. 1963), xiv.
29. Contemporary accounts of the Mongols and of European contacts with them in C. Dawson (ed.), *The Mongol Mission* (1955) and B. Spuler, *History of the Mongols* (Eng. tr. 1972). Spuler's *The Mongols in History* (1971) is a useful introductory sketch; more detail in S. Runciman, *History of the Crusades*, (1954), III, pp. 237–350 and J. J. Saunders, *History of the Mongol Conquests* (1972). The Mongol empire presented an economic opportunity to Europe throughout the thirteenth century as well as a military threat in a single year; thus the unusual and stimulating experience of seeing medieval Europe from the outside can be prolonged down to 1300 and beyond.
30. Below, pp. 93–96.
31. Their paternal grandfathers were brothers.

2 *European History: Early Modern*

Brian Pullan

Late medieval and early modern European history presents specific problems of its own, and with some of them this chapter is concerned. To begin by stating the obvious: the most impressive kind of historian at any level is the one who shows, when he looks at the past, genuine insight into the kind of world he is observing. For him the past has a concrete meaning; he writes his history in terms of people doing things or thinking things, whether those people are specific groups or outstanding individuals: and he does not reduce it to abstract formulas. He understands something both of its relevance to the present day and of the ways in which it is alien to his own world.

Few historians can study any segment of the past with intelligence and devotion if they are really convinced that it has nothing to do with the present and cannot tell them anything about permanent human problems, or about how the world came to be what it is today. If they feel that the past is quite unrelated to the present, then they will fail to apply to the interpretation of the past their own experience of the way things happen, and one of the most important constituents in historical judgment will thereby be lacking. Anybody who studies the Renaissance and the Reformation will soon find himself invited to inquire into the origins of intellectual attitudes arguably fundamental to the 'liberal' societies of western Europe in the nineteenth and twentieth centuries. Some feeling of communion with the past, some recurrent illusion that the years are falling away and the gulf of time has vanished, is indispensable to any good historian.

On the other hand, historians clearly have to cultivate a sense of anachronism. It was in the Italian Renaissance that intellectuals learnt to convey something of the distance between the ancient world and that of fifteenth-century Italy, instead of casting antiquity into the mould of their own times, and portraying its great figures as romantic and chivalrous heroes. If you study the Renaissance period, you should follow their example in recreating a world not irrelevant but certainly alien to the present day. You must bear in mind the vast gulf between a generally industrialized and a pre-industrial society, or the enormous difference between the powers available to a government which disposes of the radio and to one totally without the means of instant communication across great distances. You ought to reflect on the extraordinary sensitivity of late medieval or early modern political history to succession crises and dynastic accidents, and often remember how vulnerable to famine and disease were economies which had known no revolutions in medicine, agriculture or transport. You should try to share the mentality of people to whom the possibility of infinite material progress had never been suggested. Such exercises may help you to think yourself back into the past.

Since it is the historian's business to interpret the past to the present, it is inevitable that he should generally employ expressions which are in wide currency today. Certainly a student writing forty-five-minute essays for an examiner will be tempted to use, as a form of shorthand, expressions such as 'strong government', 'administrative centralization', 'urbanization', 'industrialization' or 'capitalism': and he will have all too little time either to define these or to hedge them round with qualifications. But these and similar terms tend to become anachronistic and empty clichés unless, at some point or other, the writer indicates the very restricted meaning which must be placed upon them when they are applied to the late Middle Ages or to the sixteenth and seventeenth centuries. Over-indulgence in such language can be cured by reflecting that in one of the most highly 'urbanized' regions of early modern Europe, the Italian territories of the Venetian Republic, in 1548 only about twenty per cent of the population lived in towns of 10,000 or more inhabitants: whereas in Great Britain in 1955 fifty-three per cent of the population lived in towns of over 50,000. You might remember, too, how town and country could mingle within town walls, and perhaps recall how in the city of Montpellier in the mid-sixteenth century more than twenty per cent of the tax-paying population were classified as peasants, and how three of its four parishes were 'saturated with country life, cluttered with dung-heaps, herds of pigs, and mule-trains picking off the pedestrians in the narrow streets'.[1] Acquaintance with some of the iconoclastic essays of Russell Major on the French Renaissance monarchy may impress on the mind a salutary sense of the practical limitations on the power of one of the proudest kings in Europe – of the sparseness of his army and civil service, of the strength of regional independence, of the might of the higher aristocracy and of the vagueness and confusion of frontiers and administrative boundaries.[2] A glance at the maps in Boris Porchnev's immense study of French popular disturbance in the seventeenth century gives some idea of the looseness of royal control over outlying provinces[3] – even at a time when Richelieu and Mazarin were supposedly building up the power of the monarchy to unprecedented heights. You should not only think about such things, but demonstrate that you have done so. Otherwise you may create the impression of being divorced from the reality of the past.

There is, unfortunately, no doubt that the prevalence of 'outline' courses in European history does encourage such a divorce from reality and a retreat into suspiciously neat generalization. Examining conventions are unlikely to encourage you to study European history with anything like the same rigour and intensity as the history of your own country. Yet it will soon be clear to you that regional privilege, local patriotism, and civic or provincial loyalties are of crucial importance to understanding European history in this period: or that Italian cities experienced the Renaissance, and German cities the Reformation, in strikingly different forms. This was an age in which cosmopolitan, exportable revolutionary programmes and international movements may be held to have played a smaller part than in the nineteenth and twentieth centuries: although in the days of Calvin and the Jesuits they were certainly not negligible, and in speaking of the time of Charles v it would be foolish to suppose that there were no international organizations, however ramshackle. Since the time to study is limited, and the time allowed to report one's findings even more so, there naturally arises a temptation to talk of kingdoms, empires or peninsulas, of 'Spain', 'France', 'Germany' or even 'Italy', as if they formed socially and politically homogeneous units, rather than 'geographical expressions', 'dynastic unions' or 'power aggregates'.[4] But such temptations must at least be controlled. We all have to reach some compromise between the pursuit of the general and the grasp of the particular, and such compromises must be a matter of individual judgement. The problem arises in an unusually acute form when trying to decide how to balance regional against general knowledge.

Excessive attention to regional peculiarities tends to destroy all structure and pattern in one's writing. Since it is impossible to establish mastery over any sector of the past without imposing upon it a form which is partly the creation of the historian's mind, lack of pattern suggests lack of control, and failure, or at least malfunctioning, of the mental digestive process. In discussing, say, the economic depression of the late fourteenth century, or the impact of the Thirty Years War on Germany, you will certainly be very much aware how different were the fates that could overtake different localities within the same country, or different groups within the same society. But you should not make the mistake of writing an extended historical travelogue, merely describing the different things that happened in different regions, and so producing either a parody of the *Cambridge Economic History* or a series of summaries of specialized articles. Every attempt must be made to view the subject as a whole and to hammer out tentative principles for your own guidance and your reader's enlightenment. On the other hand, over-stress on general matters may result in the issue of a neatly packaged but totally abstract and unreal explanation of a complicated series of past events. Be warned by the German professor in Katherine Ann Porter's *Ship of Fools,* who 'took on any subject or situation, on a moment's notice, poured it into the mould of his own mind and handed it back to you all in one piece, without a seam. . . . It took genius to be such a bore as that.'

A practical way out of the difficulty may lie in alternating, in your reading, between general works on a wide-ranging subject and a small selection of important specialized studies, which will enable you to bring generalizations down to earth and to test them on a particular sounding-board. For example, reading on the fifteenth-century Renaissance should not be confined to Burckhardt and to recent general surveys such as those of Denys Hay and John Larner, admirable as these are:[5] it ought to include one or two studies of Florence (say, Holmes and Brucker), and perhaps David Chambers's brief, much needed book on Venice.[6] Understanding of the early Reformation will be enormously enhanced by progressing beyond Hajo Holborn's *History of Germany* and trying to find out what happened when the gospel was first preached in Nuremberg, Strasbourg or Zürich:[7] to discover what one means by speaking of 'the introduction of the Reformation' into a city. Try to acquire relatively precise knowledge of the mechanics of abolishing the mass in one particular place, or of the problems involved in dissolving convents in at least one German principality; find out how the people of Zürich and Strasbourg reacted to the sermons of Zwingli or Zell. Naturally, you must be very careful not to accumulate a mass of local examples without some lynch-pin to hold them together, and Bernd Moeller's concise and strongly argued survey of imperial cities and the Reformation may provide one.[8] Similarly, study of the French Reformation and the wars of religion can gain considerably if you have at least referred to the monumental local studies by Drouot or Le Roy Ladurie.[9] Comprehension of the Counter-Reformation could certainly be increased by examining in detail the kinds of obstacle encountered by a single bishop, such as Borromeo of Milan, in his efforts to enforce the decrees of the Council of Trent:[10] although it would be difficult to make any pretence at generalization from this particular instance. In these and other fields, a skilful blending of general and particular is far more impressive and far more valuable educationally than either flatulent generality or disparate fact-grubbing. One of the additional benefits of attention to local studies is that it creates the incentive to read works in foreign languages, and to become acquainted with the un-English outlook and methods of continental historians whose writings have not been translated.

No history student presenting conclusions in the shape of brief essays can be expected to show acquaintance with the whole range of regional variations occurring within any given state or geographical unit. But he can reasonably be called upon to distinguish between the very different political and social structures of, say, Aragon and Castile, and not repeatedly conceal them beneath the blanket-like monosyllable 'Spain'. He ought, when he thinks of the United Provinces, to remember the contrasts between Holland and Gelderland, between the regions dominated by powerful cities and the Orangist zones of influence, between the areas most dominated by the Calvinists and those where the greatest variety of belief was found. He ought to realize that the level of economic development attained by northern Italy – within the quadrilateral formed by Genoa, Milan, Venice and Florence – was (then as now) far higher than that reached south of Rome and in Sicily: and he should know that the political traditions of the south, shaped by a foreign monarchy liable to succession-crises and by the extensive enfeoffment of territory, were very different from those based on the mutual cannibalism of the land-grabbing city-states of the north. And so on. Those who habitually write as though they are failing to recognize even these elementary differentiations will certainly put themselves at a grave disadvantage.

One tell-tale characteristic of the feebler kind of history student is tendency to regurgitate his history in crude lumps, which have not been broken down into units small enough to be serviceable. This points both to a poor sense of reality and to a failure of analytical power. One form of this fatal defect has already been discussed. Another – no less pernicious or treacherous – lies in addiction to a form of naive sociological generalization. It may be detected in the habit of pushing 'the nobility', 'the middle classes', 'the bourgeoisie', 'the urban proletariat' or 'the peasantry' from point to point in one's prose as if they were counters on a snakes-and-ladders board. For the sake of clear thinking, such terms need to be analysed and defined, and finer distinctions usually have to be established within these broad categories. In French history, for example, the word 'nobility' can only be a veil disguising the vast differences between landed magnates of the calibre of the Guises or the Duc de Rohan, and the ruined squireens who sometimes headed peasant rebellions in the south-west. It does not distinguish between the blue-blooded marquis and the *officier* who is technically a nobleman, but cannot get himself socially accepted by those whose nobility has been hallowed by time. Not surprisingly, statements which apply fairly well to one species of French nobleman often have little relevance to another – and you must be ready to lift the veil whenever appropriate, and demonstrate your powers of analysis and discrimination. At a time when sociological analysis is fashionable, it is vital that the sociology be convincing: and it is not good sociology to lump together wage-earning journeymen, well-to-do guild-masters, retail traders, impotent house-poor, professional beggars and peasants living inside town walls under the heading of 'the urban proletariat'. Nor should professional men, merchants, royal officials, and city rentiers be squeezed for all purposes into a category cavalierly labelled 'the bourgeoisie', and supposed to act with consistency and solidarity as a homogeneous unit. Some of the more interesting research on the social history of the Reformation does not follow 'class' lines. For example, it has been suggested that in sixteenth-century Lyons sympathy for some form of Protestantism can be related, not to 'class' or 'socio-economic position', but to vocation or trade:[11] and the person who deals only in the crudities of class will fail to appreciate this. The man who thinks only in terms of 'the middle classes' acting as a solid bloc may forget how frequently the Parlementarians and the *avocats-échevins* of the French provinces found themselves on opposite sides in moments of crisis.

All in all, the abler candidates tend to be those who prove that they can particularize without obscuring pattern or theme, and who on the other hand avoid producing over-neat and unreal generalizations. Let us imagine two students of quite markedly different ability tackling an examination question on the fashionable subject of the relationship between religious and social radicalism in the period 1520–50, and deciding to do so on roughly similar lines, involving some discussion of the social composition and teachings of the Anabaptists. The weaker man, B, contents himself with flat generalities: these are by no means completely untrue, but they do betray a certain lack of discrimination and of analytical strength. He says that Anabaptism appealed primarily to the lower classes and to the emergent proletariat of a Europe in which 'feudalism was marching with a Marxist inevitability into capitalism' (a phrase culled from a recent book on Luther and unfortunately not discarded). Because of the economic insecurity prevailing among the poor in the decade 1525–35, many Anabaptists advocated communism, and put their doctrines into practice at Münster. It was their attitude towards private property and the implied threat of social anarchy that accounted for their being so savagely persecuted, although most of them were really very peaceful people, and were in no sense revolutionary.

The abler student, A, breaks every one of these generalizations down into particles, and by so doing achieves a much more powerful insight. He points out that after its first two years, 1525–7, Anabaptism proved to have relatively little appeal for city patricians or landed aristocrats, although special circumstances tempted a number of landowners in Moravia (such as the Liechtensteins of Nicolsburg) to attract artisans of Anabaptist inclinations to their estates, and they were prepared to grant them protection. The bulk of the Anabaptists in the late 1520s and the early 1530s seem to have been quite well-to-do artisans, and peasants of almost every status from yeoman to landless labourer – though in the Duchy of Württemberg there was a marked tendency for Anabaptism to attract people of lower standing as the century advanced. Both in Switzerland and in Swabia, Anabaptism tended with the passage of time to become a movement for villagers rather than townsmen. Certainly the Swiss Brethren and the Dutch Mennonites (two of the main persuasions within Anabaptism) constantly advocated voluntary mutual aid and the responsible use of private property in the interests of the whole community. But it seems unlikely either that they practised communism or were condemned by city magistrates for doing so: although certain theologians, and especially Melanchthon, persisted in the face of all the evidence in supposing that they did. Significantly, those Anabaptists who did practise a thoroughgoing communism – disciples of Jacob Hutter in Moravia and Slovakia – were also the ones who most consistently obtained the protection of the rich and powerful. There is no denying that surviving wage-statistics and grain prices, from Flanders to northern Italy, do suggest that times were very hard in the late 1520s and early thirties. But the communism of the Hutterites cannot be explained simply as a response to hardship: their surrender of private property was a form of *Gelassenheit*, a means towards the self-abandonment of the ascetic. The Münster episode was certainly of great importance in discrediting Anabaptism, though it was as much a consequence as a cause of persecution; and the communism practised in Münster may have been the product both of abnormal siege conditions and of chiliastic doctrines which did not appeal to the general run of Anabaptists. In general, the essence of the Anabaptists' radicalism probably lay in their views on the nature of the Church and their attitude to the magistrate, rather than in their opinions on private property and its uses. Their desire for a 'separate Church' was certainly revolutionary – although it threatened revolution by withdrawal from society, rather than revolution by subversion thereof.

Not everybody will agree that A's answer is of first-class quality. But at least it reveals the critical and analytical capacity, the distrust of tidy generalization, which are conspicuously absent from B's answer: and for all its scepticism it is not completely negative.

One danger inherent in the outline course is its tendency to encourage over-generalized, facile, unrealistic writing. Another hazard lies in the tyranny of convention. The range of subjects which could be studied and examined in a substantial period of European history is enormous; no syllabus can be sharply defined, no book-list be finite. In some universities, there is no precise co-ordination between what is taught and what is examined, especially where the faculty is large and the organization of teaching decentralized. This situation can be justified by the excellent argument that one should not examine the candidate on what his lecturer, tutor or supervisor has said, but on the initiative and independence which he pesonally has shown. However, to prevent the examining of European history from becoming a game of chance or a form of shadow-boxing, certain conventions inevitably develop. It is known that there are very likely to be questions on the Hundred Years War and the Thirty Years War, on the Italian Renaissance and the Conciliar Movement, on either Charles v or Philip II, on either Luther or Calvin, on the French wars of religion or on the revolt of the Netherlands, and so on. It is usually in some such belief that the teachers and the taught place their bets before the wheel spins. There is a risk that this may discourage adventurous teaching and inquiry, because the establishment of new conventions in response to new research is a very slow process indeed: and since in English first degree courses' time is very limited, teachers are naturally reluctant to cause people to invest a lot of it in formally studying many subjects which 'may never come up'. Students, too, can be exaggeratedly conservative in their ideas about what is likely to appear in the examination paper. A sensible student will be prepared to break away from convention and develop interests of his own, reading outside the generally prescribed topics: not ignoring them, but going beyond them.

You should, in fact, bear in mind that it can be difficult for an able man to prove himself if he only answers stock questions in popular areas of study dominated by respected textbooks. Where such textbooks do exist, they tend – as do Historical Association pamphlets and other aids – to impose an orthodoxy on the subject which makes it difficult to show independence of mind. There is, of course, good reason to go on studying the revolt of the Netherlands or the Spain of Philip II, because their intrinsic importance is very great: but you should remember that the text-books which dominate the subject, excellent as they are, may need to be brought up to date and amplified – e.g. by systematic perusal of the pages of *Past and Present* and *The Economic History Review*, and by looking at a selection of specialized studies. You should bear in mind that examination papers in European history tend to consist of a number of questions located within the well-trodden areas, and of a number of others introduced as it were to show the flag – both to indicate the growing importance of a new subject, and to cater for the special interests of the more enterprising candidates. It is perhaps inevitable that only a minority will tackle the enterprising questions – but it is exasperating when seventy-five per cent of answers returned are addressed to no more than thirty per cent of the questions in the paper. Where candidates bunch together in choice of question, they may blunt the examiner's sensibilities and make it appear that their abilities are rather similar. It does occasionally happen that, in the belief that the candidates have been studying hackneyed topics at a level on which historians are no longer saying anything new or exciting, university examiners lose their tempers and eliminate all conventional questions from the paper. Luther and Louis XIV are alike expelled, to the intense indignation of the students, who have prepared themselves only for questions of that sort. To insure against such an occurrence is an act of mere prudence.

Both candidates and examiners can, perhaps, contribute to dissolving this unhappy situation. The students could be more venturesome. Nobody who allows examining convention to dominate him can expect to do well out of examinations. Examiners regularly accuse candidates of believing far too strongly in the primacy of political history and international diplomacy, and of showing comparatively little knowledge of social, economic, intellectual or 'cultural' history. Seldom do they reveal much acquaintance with anything outside the area bounded by Gibraltar and the Elbe, and after about 1530 even Italy becomes a dark subcontinent.

For their part, students could find a remedy. There is, for example, a substantial Anglo-American literature on Hussite Bohemia. Some of it (e.g. the work of Kaminsky[12]) is both tough and stimulating, and, quite apart from its intrinsic importance, may lead to a new understanding of the Reformation, which could well be seen as a continuous process stretching back into the late Middle Ages. The articles of Marian Malowist and Jerome Blum's wide-ranging treatise on Russian agrarian society do make it possible to grasp some of the main features of the social and economic history of eastern Europe and Russia.[13] Gustavus Vasa and Gustavus Adolphus, seen through the pages of Michael Roberts,[14] may have a freshness denied to Charles V and Louis XIV. Fernand Braudel's colossal survey of the Mediterranean[15] is a splendid introduction to French historical impressionism, though few would be capable of digesting it in its entirety. Furthermore, the economic history of this period is seldom of so highly technical a character that its broader principles cannot be grasped with a little trouble. Bills of exchange and devices for evading the usury laws may be somewhat daunting and the problems of regional variation are acute. But some knowledge of international commerce and finance, monopolies, inflation, population movements, and economic policies may be indispensable even to the proper understanding of primarily political history. It is true that many students understandably feel that they would have no talent for 'cultural' history, and that there is little point in studying it without first-hand acquaintance with the works of art to be discussed. However, they are not normally required by history examiners to engage in the analysis of style, but rather to consider the interplay between socio-political history and the story of art, music and literature. For those with no taste for art history, it is possible to cultivate an interest in science, medicine or technology, and in the ways in which these impinged on – or failed to affect – people's lives.

Examiners, too, might contribute to a solution. In setting questions in popular and much studied areas, they might take care to ask them in a thought-provoking form and perhaps in such a way as to require specific regional knowledge and force people to go beyond standard text-books: not the old favourite, 'Were the French Wars of Religion religious?', but something on the lines of 'Analyse the role of the peripheral provinces in the French Wars of Religion'. They might also systematically seek to raise the status of economic, social and cultural history by regularly asking large numbers of questions about them; and they might make sure of setting a certain number of highly flexible general questions which would give candidates ample opportunity to develop and demonstrate individual interests.

If one of the difficulties in the study of European history lies in the dominance of good text-books in certain areas, there is another of a contrasting character. The stress laid by examiners on the analytical and problematic naturally encourages attention to certain classic academic controversies. Was there, or was there not, a general economic depression in Europe in either the fifteenth or the seventeenth century? When did fully-fledged civic humanism first appear in Florence and how far can its advent be connected with Milanese aggression in 1402? What connections should be traced between the spread of Protestantism and the 'rise of capitalism'? In what sense was there a 'general crisis' in Europe in the mid-seventeenth century, and how far should the Thirty Years' War be blamed for it? And French peasant revolts of the seventeenth century: were they a manifestation of a straight class-struggle between the 'feudal state' and the peasantry, or were they generally led by landlords who themselves had a grievance against the king and his immediate servants?

Here there is certainly no risk that students will be tempted to rely on text-books or repeat an established orthodoxy. A cold plunge into academic confusion may have a salutary effect on someone accustomed to thinking of history as a compilation of cut-and-dried facts; and many tutors or supervisors may be eager to seize the opportunity of demonstrating how the same piece of evidence can assume a totally different significance for two different scholars. The danger is of another kind – that you may find yourself utterly separated from the materials of history by the modern scholars discussing them, and that in consequence the debate may seem as sterile as a scholastic disputation on how many angels could dance on a pin-point. You may be tempted to give a blow-by-blow account of the debates of modern historians in the pages of learned journals, rather than write about the events, situations or people of the remoter past. In your defence, you could of course argue that the word 'history' is habitually used, not merely to designate 'what actually happened', but also to denote the way in which 'what actually happened' is reconstructed or re-lived in the mind of the historian. It could be said that there are many historical concepts, the Renaissance included, which are partly the creation of historians writing in the nineteenth and twentieth centuries, and cannot be fully understood without reference to those historians. Although many examiners dislike historiography, its total exclusion from scripts and essays can hardly be justified. More basically, you could point out that it is extremely difficult to deal critically with a controversy if you have no first-hand acquaintance with the sources – and usually, in following an outline course, you have little time for these, even if they are not hidden in remote archives and libraries.

No very satisfactory advice can be given here, though one or two warnings may be issued. Examiners are seldom impressed by those who merely report a debate among scholars without expressing any critical opinion as to the value of the various contributions, or making any attempt to reconcile the conflicts of views which they are describing. Nor do they like over-acknowledgement, and the cluttering of your prose with references to Dr This and Professor That – especially where they suspect you of dropping the names of men whose work you have not actually read at first-hand. Airy and inaccurate references to 'the Marxists' are even worse, since Marxists do not always think the same way and often criticize each other. You can afford to pay the examiners the compliment of supposing that they may recognize where some of the arguments come from. Nor should you simply assume that 'latest is right', and automatically award the palm every time to the newest contribution to the debate. In general, modern scholars, however vast their learning or dazzling their panache, should not be allowed to obscure the people, events or situations with which they are concerned.

Very occasionally, a really able undergraduate historian will succeed in stepping outside and beyond the existing limits of a standard academic controversy, and cutting through all its entanglements by seeing a new issue which all the learned combatants have failed to appreciate. Flair of this kind is difficult to describe or acquire. But you can perhaps get some idea of it by studying the technique used in certain printed articles which all deal with matters of intense controversy: John Elliott's remarks on the general crisis of the seventeenth century,[16] or possibly the first sections of a brief contribution by Herbert Luethy to the debate on Calvinism and Capitalism.[17] Since it is the technique that counts, you could also refer to Jack Hexter's famous article on the dispute between the Tawney and Trevor-Roper 'schools', which, dealing with seventeenth-century England, may have much to teach the Europeanist.[18] These essays all begin with a terse account of the controversy; their object is to illuminate the most contrasting and irreconcilable viewpoints and delineate the main issues at stake – rather than to report, one after the other, the opinions of every historian who has ever had a go at the problem. After this they begin to step outside the established arena of conflict, and to draw attention to large omissions on the part of the gladiators. They raise, even if they do not always answer, questions that are too frequently ignored. Notice how Luethy, discussing the Weber thesis and its critics, says: the economic disparity between Catholic and Protestant countries had become real enough by the early seventeenth century. But should we not be asking in what ways the Counter-Reformation hindered economic development, rather than concentrating solely on how Calvinism may or may not have promoted it? Similarly Elliott asks: why assume that the cluster of 'revolutions' in the mid-seventeenth century was unique – did not an equally impressive 'general crisis' occur around the 1560s? And were these civil disturbances 'revolutions' in any commonly accepted nineteenth- or twentieth-century sense? These are examples of a skilful shifting of the grounds of argument that can be far more refreshing than any painstaking but inconclusive recitation of what has already been discussed.

Remember that the examiner may be trying to suggest to you a slightly new approach to a time-honoured problem when he puts such questions as: ' "The causes of seventeenth-century disturbances are not far to seek: what needs to be explained is their almost universal failure to produce lasting results." Comment': or, ' "In the seventeenth century, political stability, rather than civil disturbance, is difficult to explain." Discuss.' He will be pleased if you accept his invitation.

When a student, hacking his way through half-a-dozen contentious works, detects a feeling of growing dissatisfaction with a writer's general line of approach, let him stop reading at once and try to analyse his own reactions. He may be on the point of detecting an error of logic, disagreeing with an unargued basic assumption, or discerning the ways in which the debaters are at cross-purposes with one another. To criticize a writer's use of statistics or his intricate arguments about chronology, you may have to depend on the counter-testimony of another expert: in such matters, Lane is needed to question Lopez, or Seigel to upset Baron. But as far as general approach is concerned, you may be able to show independence of mind, and that impressive common sense on which all the best historical writing depends. You will notice that in the articles cited above, Hexter and Elliott in particular are not drawing on specialized knowledge but relying chiefly on common sense and a feeling for how things really happen, developed through wide experience as historians. This 'feeling for how things really happen' enables Hexter, criticizing the assumptions of debaters of the English 'gentry controversy', to put forward such statements as: 'It is *not* true that a political or social group occupying a strategic position in the power structure will necessarily and always use that position to seek supreme political power for itself.' To return to the point from which this chapter started: a cultivated intuition for the way things really happen, a grasp of what the world was and is really like, a realistic sense of the past – these are the hallmarks of a good historian at any level.

Notes

1. See Emmanuel Le Roy Ladurie, *Les paysans de Languedoc* (2 vols., Paris 1966), I, pp. 336–41.
2. E.g. J. Russell Major, 'The French Renaissance monarchy as seen through the Estates General', *Studies in the Renaissance,* 9 (1962), pp. 113–25.
3. See Boris Porchnev, *Les soulèvements populaires en France de 1623 à 1648* (Paris 1963), pp. 665–76.
4. For this last useful phrase, see Garrett Mattingly, *Renaissance Diplomacy* (Peregrine Books ed. 1965), pp. 118–9.
5. Denys Hay, *The Italian Renaissance in its historical background* (1961); John Larner, *Culture and Society in Italy, 1290–1420* (1971).
6. George Holmes, *The Florentine Enlightenment, 1400–50* (1969); G. A. Brucker, *Renaissance Florence* (New York 1969); D. S. Chambers, *The Imperial Age of Venice, 1380–1580* (1970).
7. This can be done through, for example, Hans Baron, 'Religion and politics in the German imperial cities during the Reformation', *English Historical Review,* 52 (1937), pp. 405–27, 614–33; Gerald Strauss, 'Protestant dogma and city government: the case of Nuremberg', *Past and Present,* 36 (1967), pp. 38–58; M. U. Chrisman, *Strasbourg and the Reform: a study in the process of change* (1967); Norman Birnbaum, 'The Zwinglian Reformation in Zurich', *Past and Present,* 15 (1959), pp. 27–47; R. C. Walton, *Zwingli's Theocracy* (Toronto 1967).
8. Bernd Moeller, *Reichsstadt und Reformation* (Gutersloh 1962);

also available in French translation as *Villes d'Empire et Réformation* (Geneva 1966).

9. Henri Drouot, *Mayenne et la Bourgogne, 1587–96; contribution à l'histoire des provinces françaises pendant la Ligue* (Paris 1937), I and II; Le Roy Ladurie, *Les paysans.*
10. Cf., for example, Mario Bendiscioli's account in *Storia di Milano,* Fondazíone G. Treccani degli Alfieri (Milan 1957), p. 122 ff.
11. Cf. Natalie Zemon Davis, 'Strikes and salvation at Lyons', *Archiv für Reformationsgeschichte,* 56 (1965), pp. 48–64. 'The métiers represented [among the Protestants of Lyons] involve skills and are mostly those in which something new has happened – new technology, such as printing; new claims for prestige, such as painting; and jewelry and goldsmith's work; or even newly introduced to Lyons, such as the manufacture and finishing of silk cloth. In contrast, very few grain merchants, vintners, butchers, bakers or ropemakers of *any* status became Protestants' (p. 54).
12. Howard Kaminsky, *A History of the Hussite Revolution* (Berkeley – Los Angeles 1967).
13. Cf., for example, Marian Malowist, 'The economic and social development of the Baltic countries from the fifteenth to the seventeenth centuries', *English Historical Review,* 12 (1959–60), pp. 177–89; Marian Malowist, 'Poland, Russia and western trade in the fifteenth and sixteenth centuries', *Past and Present,* 13 (1958), pp. 26–41; Jerome Blum, 'The rise of serfdom in Eastern Europe', *American Historical Review,* 62 (1956–57), pp. 807–36; Jerome Blum, *Lord and Peasant in Russia from the ninth to the nineteenth century* (Princeton, N.J. 1961).
14. See Michael Roberts, *The early Vasas: a History of Sweden, 1523–1611* (1968); Michael Roberts, *Gustavus Adolphus: a History of Sweden, 1611–32* (1953–58), I and II.
15. Fernand Braudel, *La Méditerranée et le monde méditerranéen à l'époque de Philippe II* (Paris 1966), 2 vols; Eng. trans. 1972, 1973.
16. J. H. Elliott, 'Revolution and continuity in early modern Europe', *Past and Present,* 42 (1969), pp. 35–56.
17. Herbert Luethy; 'Once again: Calvinism and capitalism', *Encounter,* 22 (1964), pp. 26–38.
18. J. H. Hexter, 'Storm over the gentry', in his *Reappraisals in History* (1961), pp. 117–62.

3 European History: Modern

Jonathan Steinberg

Lord Acton, delivering his inaugural address as a professor in June 1895, remarked that 'to historians the later part of their subject is precious because it is inexhaustible'.[1] There are few teachers of modern European history and probably fewer students who would share that view today. Advances in publishing and expansion in the number of full-time professional historians have yielded an appalling overproduction of books, articles and journals. The ordinary working historian in modern European history ought to keep up with at least a dozen journals devoted to aspects of his work. Of course, he never can, and his students even less so. One example will suffice. In the February 1971 issue of *History*, the Journal of the Historical Association, I count 9 new titles listed under 'Early Modern', of which some are in English history. By comparison there are 19 titles under 'The Eighteenth Century', of which 14 are on European history; 20 titles listed under 'The Nineteenth Century', of which 8 are European history; 33 titles under 'The Twentieth Century', of which 22 are European. And this is not the whole story, for *History*, unlike the *American Historical Review* or the *English Historical Review,* is not, in a sense, an official journal of record and can afford to be selective.

If this profusion represents the dilemma of the professional historian, the student faces the opposite one. He can see for himself in any bookshop that 'of making many books there is no end; and much study is a weariness of the flesh'. He knows that he has a week to 'do' a subject and can expect no more than forty-five minutes' worth of examination time in which to 'undo' it. For most undergraduates and sixth-formers, all the journals and new publications are irrelevant. They have to master very rapidly alien subjects for which they have no previous preparation. If they do the 'modern period' at A- or S-level, they may well do it in precisely the way that Dr Pullan has described in Chapter 2: Bismarck and Cavour can get the 'flat treatment' as easily as Charles v.[2] The average student will look with dismay at the mountains of books and turn away to find an Historical Association Pamphlet.

The profusion of writing in the modern period can be a blessing as well as a curse. The sheer number of books available on most modern topics means that nobody need ever be forced to grapple with an unpalatable authority. If you don't like Gordon on the German Army under the Weimar Republic, try Carsten or Craig or Wheeler-Bennett.[3] And why not? All tastes are not the same, and the list of 'recommended reading' was meant to help, not to cause drudgery. A wise teacher of mine once said that ideally historical or literary education should simply consist in flushing bright young men and women into libraries where lots of amiable older people would stand at the ends of the rows, whispering, 'Have you read this? It's marvellous!' The best preparation for any historical examination at any level is an insatiable addiction to books and browsing.

Of course, what you read has to be absorbed and organized, or you may end up with only a jumble of facts, figures and impressions, not a facsimile of the past you are trying to approach. Sane men do not experience the present as a meaningless confusion, nor have they done so in the past. What keeps most of us on the rails is a strong sense of time. We are convinced that one thing follows another in some recognizable pattern. We retain our identities because we remember who we were a few minutes ago or last year. The sense of time distinguishes history from the other arts subjects. Historians serve, in Goethe's phrase, 'the clock whose hands are for ever stopped'. No matter how enamoured of sociological analysis we become, we remain historians only as long as we see explanation of events over time as our main job.

The ability to use the time-dimension skilfully distinguishes the good from the not so good candidate, and it does so on several levels at once. Suppose you are writing about the Revolutions of 1848, and you write '1748' in one passage by mistake. No examiner will think twice about that, but if you write 1748 for 1848 often enough he will begin to suspect that you have very little sense of the nineteenth century as such. This may sound absurd, but it is not uncommon. I recently examined a man who wrote on European diplomacy in the mid-eighteenth century and set the wars of Frederick the Great in the 1640s, the Seven Years War in the 1650s and so on. Unless it was just an accidental slip, it illustrates an important point. Think for a moment whether '1748' or '1848' immediately produces a set of distinct images in your mind. Do you see powdered diplomats in embroidered coats standing round a table when you think of 1748? Is 1848 associated with images of barricades and horsemen riding through city streets? Take any image or jumble of images you like here, but if 1748 is simply a number or a code-sign for the end of the War of the Austrian Succession you may be in for trouble. The dates of the past should be as real as the day on which you sit your examination.

Inaccuracy is a common difficulty with dates. Most candidates get the thousands and the hundreds right but an extraordinary number go wrong thereafter. Suppose you are writing a forty-five-minute essay on the Spanish Civil War and you state that Primo de Rivera became dictator of Spain in 1922, instead of 1923, that he fell from power in January 1929, instead of 1930, but you correctly place the foundation of the Republic in 1931. You then go on to describe the vicissitudes of Spanish political history from 1931 to the revolt of the Generals in July 1936. You use much interesting evidence but you keep getting the dates wrong; the elections of December 1934 (instead of 1933) produce a swing to the right, the Popular Front wins a great victory in 1935 (instead of 1936) etc. The closer you focus your attention the more the picture is blurred by these niggling inaccuracies. Such scripts are extremely common and put examiners into difficulties. You are clearly intelligent, but your careless use of dates makes the examiner uneasy. My own reaction would vary depending on the relationship of the errors to the narrative. For example, in the case imagined above your picture is blurred but not wrong. The chain of events makes sense and roughly follows what actually occured, except that some periods get foreshortened or elongated or otherwise distorted by your habit of flinging inaccurate dates about. You get by, although with a result much lower than you ought to get, because your picture of the past flows in the right direction.

When the inaccuracies stretch over decades or reverse the order of events, the examiner must think twice. In medieval and early modern European history, errors of a century or more can occur. In the later period, which tends to be studied in less monumental slices, the equivalent sort of error is to put the unification of Germany in 1861 rather than 1871. Essays on Napoleon and the French Empire often suffer from this sort of problem, and a random assortment of dates from 1795 to 1815 is served up by many candidates. Admittedly, there are a good many battles to remember, and candidates often get Jena, Austerlitz, Eylau, Aspern, Wagram and Leipzig into the wrong order. This becomes fatal only if it distorts the course of events. The candidate can confuse Eylau with Wagram and even put the date of the Russian defeat in 1808, but he must know that there was something called the Peace of Tilsit between Napoleon and Russia as a result. If he gets the order of events wrong at this point, he cannot understand the nature of Napoleon's rule at all and, in particular, the fact that the Russians had lost only a battle, not a war.[4]

Inaccuracies are not confined to numerical errors. In a recent examination a candidate offered the following argument in an essay on the Nazi seizure of power: since the Weimar Republic had rested on the Social Democratic Party, the depression of 1929, by throwing the workers out of their jobs, turned them away from the SPD and into the arms of the Nazis. The middle classes, who had been ruined by the inflation of 1923, had already deserted the Republic. The case was intelligently and plausibly argued. It was not wholly wrong, but it was not easy to assess either. Suppose we take it apart for a moment and examine the links. Did the Weimar Republic rest on the Social Democratic Party? Largely true but oversimplified. Were the middle classes alienated from the Republic because of the inflation? Yes, but not all of them in every area in the same way for the same reasons or to the same extent. Yes, there was depression and unemployment. But did the workers turn to the Nazis? No, the areas of lowest Nazi voting strength were solid working-class constituencies. Notice how this candidate by accumulating inaccuracies and over-simplifications ends up with a picture very far removed from the realities. His conclusion must be that the Nazis took over – how is left vague – overwhelmingly, since both middle and working classes were for them. In fact, the Nazis never got more than thirty-seven per cent of the vote in a free election and arrived at power by a complicated process of intrigue, after they had passed the peak of their voting strength. He omits the communists, the army, indeed all the institutions of society, in constructing his argument.[5]

The three types of inaccuracy I have cited belong to a common category. They all result from an imperfect sense of the course of events. The story these candidates tell is either wrong, in the wrong order, against the wrong background or much too thin and oversimplified. Fortunately there is something simple and practical which can be done to cope with the problem of imperfect control of the narrative. Every time you begin a new subject, take a scrap of paper and construct a chronology of events as you read. Take the example of the Spanish Civil War again. You are reading Hugh Thomas or Gerald Brennan as an introduction,[6] never having done a thing on the Spanish Civil War before. Brennan, in giving you the background, describes the dictatorship of Primo de Rivera and says that he came to power on 14 September 1923. Write down, '14.9.1923 – Primo de Rivera assumes dictatorship.' As you read on, take down more dates, thinking each time, 'Is that important enough to put down?' When you finish reading Brennan, you may notice that he never gave, or you missed recording, the date of Primo's fall from power, so you check it in his index or go to another book for it (28 January 1930, for the record). This technique has many immediate advantages. You cannot read passively, because you have something to do – deciding whether to take down a given date or not. In that process of adding to your chronology, you are exercising historical judgement every time you ask, 'Is that important enough to put in my chronology?' The research historian does precisely the same thing amidst his mountains of archives. 'Is this document or note important enough to transcribe?' is the basic question of every historian with an archive. Thirdly, you put together your *own* causal chain of events, and it is yours, because you have selected the evidence yourself. The material has been extracted from its bedding in Brennan's argument and hence removed from his biases or omissions. When you look at your chronology, especially if it is extracted from reading several books, you will see links and time-sequences which they have either not noticed or not emphasized. In this small way, you will be doing creative historical work. Finally, you will simply be unable to make rudimentary mistakes in narrative of the kind I have described, because the chain of events will be real to you.

There is another even deeper trap for the unwary. This is the problem of the 'isms'. Modern history swarms with the grand ideas of our era: socialism, capitalism, communism, industrialism, liberalism, conservatism, totalitarianism, nationalism, absolutism, militarism, authoritarianism, professionalism, mercantilism. There are also the '-cracies' and '-ments' – bureaucracy, technocracy, literacy, democracy, plutocracy, meritocracy, enlightenment, establishment, government, disarmament etc. All of these concepts are creatures of the modern era, and if, as Dr Pullan shows, it is anachronistic to use most of them in the early modern period, it is not therefore easier to use them in their own time. The first and much the most important thing to remember about the '-isms', the '-cracies' and the '-ments' is that they are really very complicated. All of them are protean concepts with different meanings in different places at different times and in the hands of different authors or thinkers. Beware of simplistic assumptions about any of them.

The commonest of the simplistic assumptions about these large ideas is that they are things or states of being known to the men of the past. 'Colbert by his attempts to centralize the revenues helped to bring about capitalism,' wrote one recent candidate. 'The monarchs in the eighteenth century used the Enlightenment to strengthen the bases of their absolutism,' wrote another. 'Legitimacy completely disregarded nationalism,' wrote a third of the period after 1815, 'and this accounted for its failure.' These are not contemptible assertions nor are they drawn from papers which were generally of poor quality.

What they share is a tendency to turn general ideas or historians' concepts into objects of past reality. Colbert would not have known what 'capitalism' meant. Some eighteenth-century monarchs thought themselves 'enlightened'; it was a term reflecting a state of mind or level of culture, an attitude to the world. In that sense it cannot be 'used' by anybody, because it is neither an artifact nor a policy. It is what Germans call a *Weltanschauung*.[7] Frequently candidates can cope with Enlightenment or other modern '-isms' only in the narrowest of terms. Hence Frederick the Great is said to have no claim to 'enlightenment' because he failed to give his subjects political rights, as if reason cannot be applied to the 'rationalization' of a dynastic state. Finally, from the quotation on legitimacy and nationalism I must deduce that neither of the two terms has much meaning to the candidate. What, after all, is nationalism? Why and how does it arise? The assumption underlying the quotation is that it is both obvious and inevitable, whereas it is neither. If you are sure you know what nationalism is, and think that I am making heavy weather of an obvious concept, think for a minute of 'Switzerland'. Are the Swiss a 'nation'? Or merely a state composed of three 'nations'? Are the French Swiss a separate nationality?

'Technology' is another code-word to watch. Modern European history is marked by change, but the rate of change accelerates the closer you get to the present. Technological change advances irregularly. Spurts in one sector occur at the same time as lags in another. Hence at every point in the period 1648 to the present day, the material conditions, that is, the possibilities, were changing, at first slowly and then more rapidly. The railroad made the movements of armies possible on a scale unimagined in the eighteenth or early nineteenth century, but rail transport could move men only where there were rails. Beyond the railhead, they had to walk, until the internal combustion engine began to be cheap and plentiful. Firepower expanded more rapidly than mobility. Guns got bigger from 1815 to 1914, but they were still being pulled by men and horses until well on in the First World War. Radio communication made certain military operations easy which were simply inconceivable before. Had Sir Ian Hamilton, General Monash and General Stopford been supplied with three walkie-talkie sets, the British Gallipoli offensive would have succeeded and the First World War, and possibly world history, would have been changed. As it was, neither the C-in-C nor his two main field commanders ever knew that at one point both Stopford and Monash had broken through the Turkish lines and were within a hundred yards of each other, and that the Turks were surrounded.[8] The Nazi movement depended on the radio, the microphone, the electric light bulb and the searchlight at least as much as it depended on sociological factors. Hitler's movement grasped more rapidly than any of its opponents the advertising machinery of modern politics. Reflections of this kind must always underpin your arguments when you think about modern history. Men often failed to do what may seem self-evident to you, simply and solely because they lacked certain tools or techniques which we now take for granted. Essays which have the 'feel' of changing environments stand out. 'Technology' is not simply a word to be used in general essays but a reality seen at work in history.

Preoccupation with the grand ideas or 'isms' of modern history frequently leads candidates to drift away from the conventional narrative essay and to adopt an 'analytic' approach. Typical of this genre is what I think of as the 'four-factor' analysis. Here the candidate neither tells a story nor analyses large ideas. He makes laundry lists. First, there are 'economic factors', one, two, three; then there are 'political factors', one, two, three; and, of course, there are 'social factors', one, two, three. By the use of such devices he convinces himself that he has found the driving force of history. In fact, the only thing missing is the past.[9] I have never seen a factor myself, nor have I been able to get a very clear idea from the dozens of 'factor' essays I have had to read what a factor actually is. Most candidates would, I suspect, be hard pressed to tell me. The same remedy will cope with outbreaks of 'factor analysis' as with the tendency to oversimplify grand ideas. Simply ask yourself what you mean when you speak of a 'social factor'; in most cases you will see that you have merely erected a false reality between yourself and the past.

The study of modern history encourages both temptations, because unlike medieval, early modern or ancient history, most people think they know something about recent history. Candidates deliver harsh verdicts on more recent personalities with a confidence that they would never display about more remote figures. I wish I had a penny for each time I have read that Metternich 'failed to understand the force of nationalism' or that Joseph II 'failed to appreciate that his reforms were bound to provoke the nobles'. After all, the argument runs, everybody can see that nationalism was coming – indeed, it arrives a few pages further on in the Heath pamphlet. Metternich must have been pretty thick not to have seen it too. The possibility that Clemens Lothar Wenzel *Reichsgraf* von Metternich-Winneburg-Beilstein might have known more about the world of 1815, nationalism included, than an A-level candidate or a university undergraduate does not occur to them.[10] Reflections such as these have prompted me to formulate 'Steinberg's First and Second Laws of History': 'We are no smarter than our ancestors'; and 'There is a big difference between thinking about a decision and having to make it.' Liberal application of the First Law will help to cure you of a tendency to write 'failed to understand' after the names of the great men in the past. The chances are better than even that Metternich was smarter than either of us. It will also lead to the much more interesting reflection that if Metternich, who was cleverer than I am, failed to see something which I see very clearly, there must be a reason. Is it, at least in part, that he did not know what was going to happen next? Is it not also conceivable that Metternich had a shrewd idea that nationalism would beat him in the end? Is it worth considering why Metternich did not think that nationalism or liberalism was a GOOD THING? These are really quite interesting historical questions and there are many more which bubble up as soon as the past is freed from a straitjacket. The Second Law grew out of the First, and is what I think of as my 'were you there, mate?' law. How easy it is to sit in your study writing about how stupid General Joffre was in 1915 – but how hard it was to *be* General Joffre, again and again sending men out to die, working under conditions of enormous strain, exhausted, worried, armed with incomplete information and facing an enemy who seemed never to tire.[11] Do not lurch into the other extreme. There have, alas, been many stupid generals and not a few stupid professors of history, for that matter. Certainly, Metternich was smarter than I am, but I might be more humane or have a stronger sense of right and wrong. Even Metternich made mistakes. We have a right as historians to judge our ancestors – more, we have a duty to do so. But judgement must be tempered by humility.

Humility may not be a virtue which immediately springs to mind when the word examination is mentioned, but there is a sense in which good history, and hence good examination answers, cannot be attempted without it. The historian has to recognize his own limitations of time, space and talent; he has to accept that many of those about whom he writes were much greater than he; he has to accept that ultimately he can never know the truth about the past. This modesty ought to be more than skin deep. A really good candidate has discovered that he is not in the examination (a) to show how clever he is; (b) to tell all he knows; (c) to conceal bottomless ignorance with hastily-fashioned trellises of prose (or all three), but to write about the past. Except for the fact that someone else has chosen the question, writing a forty-five-minute essay on Italian fascism and writing a book about it have a great deal in common. You might say that one is a hasty sketch and the other a large oil painting. But art goes into both. As Max Liebermann, the famous German painter, remarked, 'Skizzen heisst Weglassen' ('Sketching is leaving out'). Every examiner knows the thrill, that stirring of the nerve ends, when he suddenly realizes that he is reading the work of a first-rate candidate. A fine examination answer is simply fine historical writing.

This brings me to my last observation, one so crushingly obvious that it is almost always ignored: good books are better than bad ones. As it happens, not all good books were written recently. If, therefore, you insist, as most undergraduates do, on reading only the most recent books on a subject, you will certainly read more bad books than good ones.[12] It takes long exposure to tedious, pedestrian, humourless adaptations of Ph.D. theses written during the past ten years to make one appreciate the shrewdness of A. Lawrence Lowell or the marvellous sweep of Acton. It also underlines the often forgotten truth that Marx or Bismarck were more interesting than the people who have written about them. If I had to choose between Bismarck's *Gedanken und Erinnerungen* and all the biographies, studies, monographs and articles about him, I should not hesitate to sweep all the latter into the dustbin. While it may not be all that accurate, *Gedanken und Erinnerungen* is wonderfully funny, moving, lively, in short, a work of art.[13] The number of books by historians, especially those alive today, of which that can be said can probably be counted on the fingers of one hand. This reflection brings this chapter back to where I began. If history is not fun, it is not for you. Find yourself another subject. If it is fun, do not be ashamed to show it. Forget what is safe, prudent, conventional, and if you have ideas of your own, express them. If this advice sounds risky, it is only because we, your teachers, have made such a mess of our part of the job. Ultimately, history, even in the examination room, is talking about the past, and you can do that too.

Notes

1. Lord Acton, *Lectures on Modern History* (1960), p. 6.
2. One way to get behind the cardboard cut-out which passes for Bismarck or Cavour in most examination essays is to read a good biography or (keep this one quiet; it is a very unprofessional suggestion) a good novel. You will learn ten times more about France in the 1830s from Balzac or Stendhal than you will from any text-book. Here are a few biographies that I *enjoyed* (and hence found useful): E. L. Woodward, *Three Studies in European Conservatism* (1929), (splendid on Metternich); F. A. Simpson, *Rise of Louis Napoleon* (1909); R. R. Ergang, *The Potsdam Führer: Frederick William I* (New York 1941); Werner Richter, *Bismarck* (1965); Alan Bullock, *Hitler. A Study in Tyranny* (1952), available as a Penguin Book; Isaac Deutscher, *Stalin* (1949) reprinted in Pelican Books.
3. Harold J. Gordon, *The Reichswehr and the German Republic 1919–26* (Princeton, N.J. 1957); F. L. Carsten, *Reichswehr and Politics 1918–1933* (1966); Gordon Craig, *The Politics of the Prussian Army* (1955); J. W. Wheeler-Bennett, *The Nemesis of Power: The German Army in Politics 1918–1945* (1953).
4. One way to get on top of the problem of battles is to understand the war. Military history may not be fashionable, but much of it is very well done. Two suggestions here: David Chandler,

The Campaigns of Napoleon (1967); Michael Howard, *The Franco-Prussian War* (1961).

5. The literature on the Nazi seizure of power is immense and growing ominously larger every day. Here are a few of the many excellent titles available in English: A. J. Nicholls, *Weimar and the Rise of Hitler* (1968) in Macmillan Paperback edition. Short and elegant introduction. A. J. Nicholls and Erich Matthias, *German Democracy and the Triumph of Hitler. Essays in Recent German History*, St Antony's Publications, 3 (1971). This important collection gives you a painless introduction to some recent research. Karl Dietrich Bracher, *The German Dictatorship. The origins, structure and consequences of National Socialism* (1971). This massive book represents the mature judgement and vast learning of Germany's foremost expert on these problems. The translation is adequate.
6. Gerald Brennan, *The Spanish Labyrinth* (1943 and 1969); Hugh Thomas, *The Spanish Civil War* (1961).
7. If you can read German, you can get an excellent impression of what 'Enlightenment' meant in daily life from Goethe's autobiography – *Dichtung und Wahrheit* (Goldmanns) ed., Munich 1962), (tr. J. Oxenford, 1971); W. H. Bruford, *Culture and Society in Classical Weimar* (1962) will do the job almost as well. This is a wonderful study of life in the territory of one of the most 'enlightened' of despots.
8. Two good books on this: Alan Moorehead, *Gallipoli* (1956); Robert Rhodes James, *Gallipoli* (1965).
9. It is sometimes a good remedy for an attack of 'factoritis' to read some history written before 'factors' were invented. I like to recommend A. Lawrence Lowell, *The Government and Politics of Continental Europe*, II (Cambridge, Mass. 1896, revised and reissued many times). Lowell, who came from the most patrician of Boston families, was interested in how governments actually worked, who did what and how. It is the easiest and most useful introduction to the governments of France, Germany, Austria-Hungary, Italy and Switzerland in the nineteenth century. The questions he asks have now become unfashionable, but they remain as important as ever.
10. A good book on Metternich is Enno Kraehe, *Metternich's German Policy* (Princeton, N.J. 1963). This fascinating book studies the shrewd and supple way Metternich coped with German nationalism.
11. Try reading John Terraine, *Douglas Haig, The Educated*

Soldier (1963). After that, see how many bright ideas you have for ending the First World War easily.

12. For example, the most stimulating book on Germany before 1914 was actually written before 1914. Thorstein Veblen, *Imperial Germany and the Industrial Revolution* (New York 1914, revised and reissued 1954). It is hard to beat Karl Marx: *The Eighteenth Brumaire of Louis Napoleon Bonaparte* in *Marx-Engels Selected Works*, I, II, (Moscow 1962) or A. de Tocqueville, *L'ancien régime et la révolution* (1856) (trs. Stuart Gilbert, Fontana Paperback edition).
13. There is an English translation under the title *Reflections and Reminiscences*, which is a handy selection, ed. T. S. Hamerow, Harper Torchbooks (paperback) (New York 1968). A useful German paperback edition of selected writings is *Bismarck. Mensch und Staat* (List Bücher, Number 74).

4 *English History: 12th to 17th Centuries*

Margaret Bowker

Few periods have enjoyed more popularity for sixth form history syllabuses than the 'The Tudors and Stuarts'. As a result, university students often come to them with a feeling that there is a bed-rock of accepted fact which will provide all that is necessary for a degree. This may take such forms as '1485 saw the beginnings of a new monarchy, based on the use or help of new men', or '1530–40 saw events taking place which were the result of a revolution in government, itself the brain-child of Thomas Cromwell.' One of the most difficult transitions that the undergraduate has to make, therefore, is that from certainty to uncertainty. The bed-rock has to be seen to be sand, and shifting sand at that, which owes its apparent firmness to a whole host of assumptions which he has accepted, but which in reality scholars are constantly criticizing.

If we look critically at the first example given, the association of the year 1485 with new beginnings, we find that the monarchy of Henry VII could only be called 'new' in any deeper sense than that of there being a new king on the throne, if the power claimed for or exercised by the monarchy was new, or if it was regarded in a new way. Was it? Certainly Henry VII succeeded to the throne in an abrupt fashion, by battle; but this was not new: while primogeniture had been the custom, there had been exceptions, particularly in the late fourteenth and fifteenth centuries, and an Italian describing affairs in England in 1500 could say with some truth:

> This kingdom has been for the last 600 years governed by one king, who is not elected but succeeds by hereditary right. Should there be no direct heir, and the succession be disputed, the question is

often settled by force of arms... and therefore it has always been an understood thing that he who lost the day lost the kingdom also.[1]

Henry IV (1399–1413), the first Lancastrian king, succeeded in this way, and so did Edward IV (1461–83). Nor was there anything novel about the coronation of the first Tudor: the Yorkists had revived some older customs such as the *regiae laudes*, the veneration of the king, and the even older practice of crown-wearing.[2] But these ceremonies had a long history, and it is hard to make a case for the novelty of either the Yorkists or the Tudors in this respect. Similarly, if we look at the Council under Henry VII and his Yorkist predecessors we find that in work and composition the two were almost identical: more than half the Yorkist councillors still alive in 1485 were used by Henry VII. The councillor who was thought to had had most influence on Henry VII was Reginald Bray,[3] but he too owed his inital appointment in the royal service to Yorkist patronage.[4] The idea that Henry VII created 'a new financial system'[5] has also been subject to reappraisal as more work has been done on the financial administration of his predecessors; it was the Yorkists, and not the first Tudor, who reverted to the thirteenth-century practice of using the treasurer of the household to receive money, and they appointed the first receivers-general and special auditors for newly-acquired lands;[6] and there are strong grounds for supposing that Henry VII took some time to appreciate their policy and to adopt it.[7] The revival of the feudal incidents of wardship and marriage, in particular, which were to play such an important part in Tudor finance, was pioneered by the Yorkists in the duchy of Lancaster.[8] The dramatic picture of the Wars of the Roses toppling the feudal nobility as they 'lost their leaders on the battlefield or the scaffold'[9] has been replaced as research has revealed the large number of pardons granted by the Yorkists and Henry VII to members of noble households. Nor did their power suddenly diminish, for the practice of allowing the great families to retain men (with the result that they could have small armies at their disposal) survived into the sixteenth century unimpaired.[10]

So the rock of the 'new' monarchy of Henry VII crumbled under scrutiny. Another orthodoxy replaced it; the idea that the novelty of this period lies not with Henry VII and the dying years of the fifteenth century but with Henry VIII and a brilliant minister, Thomas Cromwell.[11] But this too is currently undergoing reappraisal, and here, once again, the ground is anything but firm. It is therefore vitally important to be aware of current assumptions and the evidence on which they rest, and also to realize how our understanding of this evidence is constantly changing as new research provides more information and asks different questions.[12]

Once the leap into uncertainty has been made, the student has taken the first step towards the academic study of history. The problems which then confront him are great, but once he has grasped that he is not learning a set of known facts but trying to interpret a great variety of different sorts of evidence in order to achieve an appraisal of men in time (which will in its turn be surpassed), he is more than half-way into his subject. This is not in the least to underestimate the problems of interpretation and assessment which then confront him. Human affairs themselves are complex, and so those who study them must grasp their complexity and find their meaning without sacrificing clarity.

The Middle Ages provide a particular kind of challenge in this respect, since the material which has survived may sometimes be slight, and the temptation to oversimplify may consequently be all the greater. Yet complexity there always is, as we can see where material in fact survives. What, for instance, are we to make of the struggle between Thomas Becket and Henry II (1154–89)? We must begin by trying to understand the characters of the principal participants in the struggle, notably the bishops, and the relationship between two institutions which nevertheless comprised the same people, the Church and the government. It was the developments within the Church and the extension of governmental activity which provided the setting for the dramatic clash between Becket and Henry II: to what extent could this clash have been avoided?

It is easy to attribute the *impasse* reached between Becket and Henry II either to their personalities (and dramatists like Eliot and Anouilh have done much to emphasize this explanation) or to an inevitable conflict between an increasingly powerful and centralized Church and a monarchy aware of the need to increase its own power if order was to be maintained. In reality neither explanation quite holds good to the exclusion of the other. It is abundantly clear that Henry II was conscious not only of the extent to which the monarchy had lost land, and therefore income, as a result of the disorders of Stephen's reign – in Oxfordshire alone it seems to have lost more than half of the royal manors – but that disorder would continue for as long as lands and goods were not protected by adequate royal courts. Henry II's attempts to find good sheriffs, however unsuccessful in the long term,[13] and his judicial reforms[14] indicate his concern for these central problems and his appreciation of the powers implicit in Angevin kingship.[15] But it was not only the monarchy which perceived the need for centralization and a measure of uniformity.

Exactly the same process was at work in the Church. Under the influence of the reforming ideals of Gregory VII (1073–85), a series of councils had been held between 1125 and 1151 which aimed at providing closer supervision of such things as ordination, the provision of benefices and tithes; at the same time the canon lawyers were giving legal authority to this control by compiling and assessing papal letters and decrees, and in so doing they tended to emphasize the supremacy of Rome. Though there was no one single canon law book which commanded total acceptance, and canon lawyers are known to have used at least fifty between 1170 and 1210, the insistence that the papacy was 'the centre and origin of ecclesiastical order'[16] was not denied even by Henry II in his attempts to restrict appeals to Rome.[17] But the primacy of Rome presented problems of a practical kind to a king and his clergy. For the clergy, in 1199, there was the novel request for papal taxation from which only a king could shield them. For the king and his subjects, there was the fear of an ever-increasing volume of litigation being adjourned to Rome, with consequent delay and expense. The king could not stand aside when cases which concerned land-ownership or which implicated his most mighty subjects were debated at Rome: he had an obligation to see that justice was done in his land and could not afford to risk losing control over his subjects. At Clarendon in 1164, therefore, Henry tried to limit appeals to Rome, and at Avranches in 1172 he insisted that appeals could be made to

Rome 'so long as, if any persons were suspect to (the king), they would guarantee not to seek to harm him or his realm'.[18] His successors took the same attitude.[19] Similarly, if the king was to ensure to his subjects any kind of order, he could not tolerate a claim to benefit of clergy which might allow a clerk guilty of murder to escape effective punishment and to repeat his offence. Henry II's attempt at Clarendon to see that clergy guilty of offences against the law of the land were punished by being unfrocked and handed over to the secular courts (in Becket's eyes the infamous double punishment) was an attempt to create order.

It would be easy to see all the necessary ingredients for a clash in these distinct and sometimes rival claims; but it would be wrong. The Church and the state were not two distinct entities poised for a fight like wrestlers in the ring; for the personnel of each were the same: the king was a churchman, just as much as the bishops were members of his realm and frequently his civil servants. In practice, the fact that many royal judges were also Henry II's bishops made conflict between the claims of ecclesiastical and secular government less likely. The canonists might urge upon the bishops the necessity of assuring themselves that the right patron presented a man to a living, usually a parish church; the king at Clarendon insisted that if a dispute were to arise about a presentation, then the royal courts and not the ecclesiastical courts should decide it. A bishop could refuse to admit a candidate to a parish and so render void in effect the decision of the royal court about the right of presentation; similarly the king could issue a whole series of writs which commanded the bishop that he *should* admit a certain patron's nominee. An *impasse* was possible. But when the men writing the writs turned out in fact to be bishops themselves, and when the question facing them was whether to hear a case in their capacity as royal judges or in their capacity as diocesan bishops, the niceties of canon law became academic and compromises were the inevitable outcome.[20] The purist's ideal of bishops chosen by the papacy without reference to the secular power ran contrary to common sense and expediency: while bishops held land, the king needed to be sure of their loyalty, and clergy and religious alike looked to the crown and the laity for financial support. The realities of the situation in the twelfth century required that the claims of the canonists for the papacy be taken with a large pinch of salt.

So why did Becket, who had himself seen the problems which confronted Henry II in his attempt to achieve a measure of order when he had held the position of chancellor, give up this office and from the see of Canterbury take issue with the king? His successors, notably Hubert Walter, possibly profiting from his example, took the way of compromise. His contemporaries on the episcopal bench were by no means unanimous in his support. Of these the most notable was in many ways Gilbert Foliot, bishop of London. He had enjoyed a good reputation as abbot of Gloucester and bishop of Hereford before his translation to the see of London; his opposition to Becket's actions, therefore, poses particular problems. Is the line separating Foliot from Becket that between the diplomat and the man of principle? If we adopt this interpretation, we leave many loose ends in the story. Why was Thomas so late in displaying his principles? Why had he to become archbishop to find them? Is this one of those occasions when an historical character can only be understood if we accept that, though his characteristics and features remain recognizable, 'his aims, his ideals, his sense of values, and his directive strength of will may have changed entirely'?[21] This is certainly the interpretation of the archbishop given by Professor David Knowles, who has studied him with perception and care over a long period.[22] Gilbert Foliot and his supporters are almost as difficult to interpret. Why did Foliot refuse obedience to Thomas? Was this because he had wanted the see of Canterbury himself? Why was he so implacable an opponent of Thomas? Was this again for personal reasons, or was it because he was as dedicated in the defence of compromise as Thomas was in defence of what he thought was the liberty of the Church? The answer will vary according to the weight given to the grounds of dispute, to 'the liberty of the Church'. Thus Foliot, like Thomas, is apt to be a battle-ground between Protestant and Catholic historians.[23] Our estimate of the man is determined to a considerable extent by our estimate of his situation; our estimate of the situation itself leads us inexorably to the study of the men involved.

The complexity of the subject is enormous and may even lead us to Camden's conclusion (when a particular historical problem had defeated him), 'to search more curiously into these matters, were nothing else but to hunt after the windes'.[24] The dispute between Becket and Henry II highlights this complexity, partly because enough evidence has survived about it. Human problems rarely prove to be simple when enough is known about them, and an historian in search of simplicity may find himself writing superficial history which makes the men of the past something less than men.

There are thus real dangers involved in ignoring, or in overlooking, the complexities which lie behind apparently simple situations. The appearance of simplicity can arise, all too easily, from a failure to cope adequately with the problem of too little evidence. Yet equally, on the other side, the survival of considerable evidence can pose its own problems, and the historian has to learn to recognize and handle these as well, even when his predecessors have not always done so. The reign of Henry III (1216–72) is apt to daunt and discourage the student simply because the number of issues to be considered, the amount of material which appears to require scrupulous attention and the detailed nature of most of the books, leave him unable to see the wood for the trees, or to distinguish the major from the minor issues. The reign was a long one, spanning some fifty-six years; it also saw some important developments in administration, notably in the exchequer under the guidance of Peter des Rivaux.[25] Enquiries were made into charters; attempts were made to see that the king supported himself from his own lands and these, if successful, would have had the effect of removing from the baronage such small say as it had in government since the need to obtain its consent, in council, to taxation would not have arisen. But the period also saw the failure to make the king financially independent, and by 1242 the baronage were refusing taxation, or, as in 1244, linking the grant of taxation with reform.

But what precisely was the reform required? It was apt to find expression in the demand that the king should take advice only from his *natural* councillors, his baronage, and in the complaint that Henry III made too much use of foreigners. But in fact there were very few foreigners in the royal service, and the king had never accepted the right of any one group to form his council. The demand that taxation should have common consent had been made in 1215 in the Articles of the Barons[26] and in Magna Carta some attempt had been made, possibly by the king himself, to define that consent.[27] But this clause was never included in the reissues of the charter under Henry III.[28] So we are left wondering why the reign was marked by so much baronial discontent which finally erupted in 1258.

In that eruption we have another opportunity to try to discover the causes of the discontent: was the complaint directed solely against an irresponsible and inefficient king who by a vow made in 1253 had committed his country to the conquest of Sicily, which would have vastly over-strained English resources? Or was the king's involvement with Sicily, and his eventual commitment to pay papal debts, simply the occasion which drove him into the hands of his baronage and enabled them to effect reforms of another kind? The sequence of events suggests that this is a possible interpretation: in 1258 the king gave his assent to the reform of the state of the kingdom (*statum regni*) and the election of twenty-four who were to work for it by scrutinizing the grievances listed by the barons at a Parliament held at Oxford. These grievances are not directed against the form of the government but against its practical shortcomings: complaints are made that the feudal right of wardship has been abused, that castles in future should be given to faithful men and not to foreigners, that heiresses and widows, whose marriages were in the king's gift, should not be married in a way which disparaged their social standing, and that the sheriffs should not misuse their courts nor their rights to take purveyance, nor take or demand money for imprisoning criminals. The barons indicate that there is a shortage of knights for assizes, and complain that they are being deprived of their tenants' services by a prevalent legal device: a tenant would make a gift to a third party who would fail to render the service due, but the third party's goods could not be confiscated for this failure, since the service was owed not by him but by the tenant. Do these grievances really indicate the extent of the discontent, or were they a cover for something else? In the sequence of events which followed, it looks as though grievances were as varied as participants in the struggle.

There was considerable delay in meeting the grievances. The twenty-four made proposals for governmental changes embodied in the Provisions of Oxford, which made the chief officers of state (the justiciar and the chancellor) annual appointments, provided that sheriffs be men of substance and that three parliaments a year should be held to which representatives of the commonalty should come to discuss the needs of the realm. The king accepted the Provisions, but the outstanding question remained: what precisely were the needs of the realm? The Provisions had done nothing specific about those put forward by the Oxford Parliament, and when, by October 1259, it was clear that reform was not forthcoming, discontent manifested itself in the revolt of a group known as the bachelors. Who they were we do not know, but their revolt makes it clear that 'reform' meant different things to different people: to the earl of Gloucester it meant that he should be allowed to go his own way without royal or baronial interference; to the council it meant a series of provisions known as the Provisions of Westminster.[29] Disunity gave the king the opportunity to resume the government of his country himself, and the pope absolved him from his oath to stand by the Provisions. He celebrated the occasion by depriving the justiciar of his office and replacing many sheriffs. In the years that followed, with the attempts at compromise and the gradual drift into civil war, each 'side' was forced to recognize that the only way to reform the realm was to control the crown; that the complaints about counsel, sheriffs and the corruption of local government would diminish only if there were a government willing to accept the challenge they presented – that it was not enough, for instance, just to insist upon the king summoning a council to agree to taxation or upon the justiciarship and chancellorship being annual offices, for the very simple reason that *the king was not bound to use them.* Was this constitutional reality recognized in the flurry of events, the proposals and counter-proposals, the mixture of motives which characterizes both Henry III and the man who emerged as his chief adversary, Simon de Montfort?[30] In a poem written after the battle of Lewes in 1264 the issue is stated in just these terms:

> Lo! we are touching the root of the perturbation of the kingdom of which we are speaking, and of the dissension of the parties who fought the said battle.... The king, with his men, wishes thus to be free: and so (it was urged on his side) he ought to be: and he must cease to be king, deprived of the rights of a king, unless he could do whatever he pleased; it was no part of the duty of the magnates of the kingdom to determine whom he should prefer to his earldoms, or on whom he should confer the custody of castles, or whom he should have to administer justice to the people, and to be chancellor and treasurer of the kingdom. He would have every one at his own will, and counsellors from whatever nation he chose, and all ministers at his own discretion....

Here, then, in the heart of the dispute, we have a poet who was also a constitutional historian *par excellence*; he has seen through the morass of detail to the central point: that it may be no use trying to reform abuses which emanate from the government; it is the government itself which must be reformed, the king and the king alone must be the subject of attack. Not for him a long-winded rehearsal of the painful means by which king and baronage were brought face to face with the stark fact that 'He who is truly king is truly free.'[31]

The ability to highlight a central point of this kind presupposes other skills, which are only acquired with time and attention to detail. If we are not to impose a wholly arbitrary interpretation upon the past, but attempt to see what interpretation the material at our disposal compels on us, we have to pay very great attention to the nature of the evidence which has come down to us. We must try to see exactly what weight it will bear. For a long time historians believed that Henry IV (1399–1413) had a parliamentary title to the throne, and that his accession 'made the validity of a parliamentary title indispensable to royalty'.[32] Stubbs' belief in a 'parliamentary title' coloured his whole view of the Lancastrians and was determined by, and itself further determined, his ideas about Parliament in the later Middle Ages. He chose to emphasize the limits which were gradually placed on the exercise of royal power. Not only had the king become limited occasionally by a council of his magnates, assembled when he chose to ask them for money (as under Henry III), but an assembly representative of the community, the Lords and Commons, had of itself achieved sufficient power to take the throne from one king, Richard II (1377–99), and give it to another, Henry IV. Only gradually did scholars realize that the evidence on which Stubbs and others had based their argument, the 'record and process' of 30 September 1399, incorporated in the Rolls of Parliament, was drawn up deliberately to deceive and could not be taken on its face value at all.[33] Once this was recognized, Professor Wilkinson could go even further and show that not only did Henry IV not possess a parliamentary title to the throne, but that Parliament did not see itself as an entity distinct from the crown and as such able to depose one king and give the throne to another; in the words of the *Modus Tenendi Parliamentum*, 'The king is the head, the beginning and the end of parliament.'[34] It had no power to act against a king, and a parliamentary title 'was outside the practical possibilities offered to a successful rebel'.[35] So an awareness of the foundation, the evidence, on which an historical argument is based is of fundamental importance to a student of history. He will rarely, if ever, be able to show that a document, fundamental to the whole interpretation of an epoch, is 'cooked' or forged. But what he will constantly have to do is to ask himself whether the evidence used to support an argument is of a kind suitable to that argument. Recent research on the Reformation in England again highlights exactly this point.

Men like Simon Fish in *A Supplication for the Beggars* were exceedingly outspoken in their criticism of the Church in England in the early sixteenth century. He criticized the clergy for taking tithes, for their immorality – 'they apply themselves . . . to have to do with every man's wife, every man's daughter and every man's maid'[36] – and for their lack of education. His criticism is echoed in the writings of Thomas More, of Colet and of Thomas Starkey,[37] and we know that the parliament of 1529, which proved to be the parliament which severed the link with Rome, was concerned enough about the non-residence of parochial clergy, and about the fees taken for proving wills and granting probate, to pass legislation about it.[38] But what exactly does this prove? Certainly that there was a desire to reform the Church among members of the House of Commons, and that there was considerable criticism of it, particularly among the better-educated members of the community. But it is easy to make the transition and to assume that if men said the clergy were immoral, then they were; that if men thought that the standard of education prevailing amongst the clergy was too low, then it was. At this moment we are placing on one kind of material more weight than it can stand. We are, in fact, making the sort of assumption made if we believe that the account of an event given by a newspaper is absolutely accurate. It may or may not be. To ascertain whether the *Supplication* is accurate or not, we need to ask not simply 'What did men think of the Church?' but 'Is there evidence which might enable us to test their opinions: evidence which might tell us what standard of education was actually attained by the clergy, how many of them were resident and how many immoral?'. Such evidence *does* survive, and suggests that it is in fact a mistake to confuse criticism of the state of the Church with the state of the Church itself. It emerges that there was a good deal of non-residence in the parishes, but that this did not result in any appreciable neglect of the cure of souls, since curates performed the duties of the incumbent as efficiently as the incumbent would in all probability have done. There was some immorality, but not on the scale that Simon Fish suggested, and though the standard of education was not high by the criteria of the humanist it was high enough to satisfy most parishioners.[39] So far, detailed studies of this kind have been done only for certain regions, and we may find that the state of the Church differed markedly from place to place. Even if this proves so, we have still to distinguish clearly between what some men thought about the Church and what the state of the Church really was. Such a distinction does not invalidate the opinions of men like Simon Fish; his opinions, even if shown to be exaggerated, remain opinions vehemently held by him and others.

The question which now emerges is why Fish, and others like him, were so vehement. Was the state of the Church – whatever that may in fact prove to be – worse by the sixteenth century, or had the level of tolerance of abuse dropped? To answer this kind of question a number of quite different approaches suggest themselves. It would be instructive to discover what experience Fish and the members of the Reformation Parliament had had of the workings and abuses of the Church. Did they come from parishes which were abnormally bad? Had they all spent a certain time in London where things may have been different? Was it fashionable to say such things in certain circles? Is there any evidence that the reform of the Church had begun before the 1530s, and that as men became more aware of the demands of the gospel, so they became less tolerant of those who did not live up to those demands?[40] What was the state of the Church in the fifteenth century, and how does it compare with that in the sixteenth century? Some of these questions will in time receive answers; some will not. But what is undeniable is that opinions like those of Fish, for whatever reasons they were held, had a very important effect on the English Reformation: for Henry VIII used the anti-clericalism of the Commons to frighten Convocation into submission and to inhibit the bishops from protesting against the supremacy.[41] It is also clear that the actual state of the parishes of England, rather than the opinions men had of them, mattered when the legislation enacted by the Reformation Parliament and its successors required enforcement. The king looked to the clergy to preach suitably about the royal supremacy and to explain to their parishioners such things as the Ten Articles and the royal Injunctions that accompanied them. The education of the parish priest, and his own financial security (or lack of it), might considerably affect his attitude to the royal commands, and this would appear to be borne out by a study of the individual priests who took discontent far enough to defy the king by participating in the Pilgrimage of Grace.[42]

It is of the utmost importance, therefore, that the student of history attend to the nature of his evidence to make sure that the weight he puts upon it is not too great. This is of particular relevance today as the questions which historians wish to ask of their material, the things which they want to know about the past, become more and more sophisticated. The questions which any one historian asks vary according to individual taste and inclination, but they also suggest themselves, to a considerable degree, by the advances which his colleagues are making in other fields – in psychology, sociology and anthropology, for instance, or, more recently, in cybernetics (particularly systems analysis). It is likely that an increasing use will be made, by academic historians, of methods and of conclusions derived from these disciplines; and if this is done, it will have to be on a much more sophisticated level than hitherto. It will be part of the would-be historian's job to see that this is so, and he will also have to see that theory is not used as a substitute for evidence (which results at best in conjectural history) but as a tool with which to elucidate it.

The problems of understanding the personality of Elizabeth I (1558–1603) provide an example of the possible opportunities for the historian to apply insights drawn from psychology, but also of the pitfalls which may await him if he does so without rigid attention to the limitations of his evidence. Elizabeth's seemingly innumerable marriage-schemes and her ultimate failure to marry pose some interesting questions for the psychologist. Had the execution of Elizabeth's own mother and the subsequent execution of Katherine Howard made such an impression upon her as a child that she was unable to tolerate the idea of marriage and child-bearing? Do the contemporary accounts of rages, tears and anger alternating with sweetness and flattery indicate a case of hysteria? The victims of this form of mental illness are sometimes sexually inadequate and frequently demand an inordinate amount of attention to compensate for the lack of love in their early years. It is absolutely right and proper to ask whether Elizabeth was a hysteric and whether her failure to marry was due to some form of psychological block. The question has been asked and answered by some historians in the affirmative.[43] But does this interpretation do justice to the material? Clearly we can achieve insight into Elizabeth's personality only from what she said and did and wrote, or from reports about her. If she was absolutely free to do as she pleased, then obviously considerable importance attaches to her actions, especially to her failure to marry. But how free was she? If she had never had the opportunity to marry anyone at all, then it would be a mistake to argue that her failure to marry was due to a defect in personality. The greater the area of choice open to any one person, the more significance we may place on the choice made. The question, therefore, of the significance which attaches to Elizabeth's failure to marry may resolve itself into a question of deciding the area of choice which we believe she had; this in turn requires that we attend to all the circumstances which determined the range of her choice.

Theoretically she could have married anyone she chose; she was 'the best marriage to be had in Europe'.[44] But in practice her choice was severely limited by a number of different factors: the first was that she was a firm Protestant, and would not change her faith nor risk submitting her realm to a religious division which in Europe had been the occasion of war; this meant that a marriage to Philip II of Spain or to the Emperor's son, the archduke Ferdinand, was out of the question, as was marriage to the duke of Anjou; all were intransigent on religion. Equally all were foreigners, and as such a cause of much alarm amongst the English: the dangers of a Spanish match were apparent under Mary (1553–58) and had been witnessed by Elizabeth;[45] the hostility of Englishmen to a foreign match was revealed when the duke of Alençon seemed to be about to marry Elizabeth in 1579. John Stubbs wrote his pamphlet entitled 'The Discovery of a Gaping Gulf whereinto England is like to be swallowed by another French marriage, if the Lord forbid not the banns by letting her Majesty see the sin and punishment thereof';[46] and when Elizabeth attempted to assert herself against the views of her subjects by arresting Stubbs and punishing him by cutting off his right hand, the culprit, before passing out, called 'God save the Queen'. The London crowd watched the scene in ominous silence. The precarious balance of power in Europe required that Spain and France were played off against one another, and that France did not dominate Scotland through an alliance with Mary Queen of Scots. This again limited Elizabeth's choice: to marry a French prince might well serve the purpose of neutralizing the danger from Scotland, but it would almost certainly incur the wrath of Spain, and after the Massacre of St Bartholomew in 1572 it would have appeared that Elizabeth, for the sake of marriage, had sacrificed the Protestant cause for a French match. There were better ways of dealing with Scotland than this; in any case, the disinclination of the duke of Anjou, and then the death of the duke of Alençon, put an end to French courtship.

In this situation, an English match may seem to have been the obvious way out; but the only candidate who was of Elizabeth's age and religion was Robert Dudley, earl of Leicester. He had shared Elizabeth's misfortunes on more than one occasion, and the two certainly had a great affection for one another. But at the beginning of the reign Robert was married. The rumours that he was going to murder his wife, and the subsequent scandal which attached to her death, effectively ruled out Leicester as a candidate. To marry him, Elizabeth would have had to risk alienating her nobility (which, as Mary Queen of Scots was to discover, could result in rebellion and even the loss of the crown), and a scandal which certainly did not accord with her idea of monarchy. Her affection for Leicester is clear; in the state of semi-consciousness which accompanied her attack of small-pox, when she thought she was going to die and regal reserve was temporarily thrown to the winds, Elizabeth spoke of Leicester.[47] Of the other English candidates, only two were canvassed; one was the earl of Arundel, who was old enough to be her father and did not possess her wit or sensitivity; the other was Sir William Pickering, who was also on the old side and whose low birth and pretentious ways threatened to unite the nobility against the match.[48] So Elizabeth was in a cruel dilemma: to keep the balance of power in Europe, and to prevent England becoming entangled in continental war, she needed to appear open to marriage; it was a diplomatic trump card, and of particular value when Mary Queen of Scots was also in the market. But to keep religious unity in her realm and to retain the love of her subjects, it was essential for her to marry from amongst the English. If this was not to divide her nobility, her choice must light on one of rank, and no such one existed unless it was Leicester, and he could be deemed an upstart. The death of his wife ruled him out. It was one thing for Elizabeth to be called a bastard by hostile powers and accordingly denied her right to the throne, it was quite another for her to lend substance to the taunt 'What religion is this, that a subject shall kill his wife, and the Prince not only bear withal but marry with him?'[49] So we must ask 'Had Elizabeth *any* choice but to remain single?' Can we infer, in the immensely difficult circumstances of her reign, very much about her personality simply from the failure of all her courtships? How far, in fact, in her case, are the insights drawn from psychology of help? Is the evidence of a kind which makes a psychological theory of her character possible?

Theories derived from other disciplines have also been used to help solve other kinds of problem. One of the most notable is the problem of the English Civil War. Why did it take place? The Marxist interpretation of class conflict has been offered as a possible answer: the Civil War was a bourgeois revolution and a stage in thc overthrow of the feudal structure, especially its monopoly of the means of production.[50] But among English scholars this interpretation has not been accepted; it appears to ignore the inherent complexities which have been revealed by investigations into the backgrounds of the members of the Long Parliament, made in the hope of establishing the similarities and differences in the social and economic fortunes of the two parties as illustrated by their adherents in the House of Commons. The results of one such investigation dramatically revealed the limitations of the method, though the limitations may well prove to be those of its practitioners rather than those of the method itself. Brunton and Pennington, in their study of the Royalists and Parliamentarians of the Long Parliament, were driven to conclude that the divisions did not correspond to economic and social differences, and that the only appreciable difference between the Royalists and their adversaries was that they were younger.[51] Their conclusions may be criticized on a number of different grounds: it may be objected that members were analysed into groups of family, patronage, economic interest, region, age and profession, but that these categories have only limited use in a period of acute political crisis when 'fundamental' issues were at stake. This at least was Sir Lewis Namier's view in his study of eighteenth-century politics. It would be necessary to examine ideological groupings – which was not done, simply because it was assumed that the ideology *must* have a relationship with background.[52] It may prove to be the case that men of republican attitudes *did* have certain other matters in common, but this will probably not come to light if we seek to ascertain similarity and difference by such crude questions as 'How many lawyers were there on each side?' and 'How many merchants?'. It may well prove relevant to ask 'What sort of lawyer?' and 'What sort of merchant?' became a republican.

Indeed Christopher Hill and Valerie Pearl have suggested that there were divisions in ideology and that these did have a relationship to background. Nearly all thc highly privileged aldermen of the City of London sided with the king, for instance, while the much less privileged citizens represented in the Common Hall were Parliamentarians; indeed, Mrs Pearl suggested that sympathy with the Royalist policy was confined in the City to the leaders of the municipality, some City officials and some of the wealthiest citizens.[53] If the background of the participants can be shown to have a similarity, then it may become possible to test more accurately than hitherto the hypotheses put forward in a variety of forms by Professor Trevor-Roper, the late Professor Tawney and Professor Stone that the financial difficulties of a number of the English gentry may explain their readiness to take up arms.[54]

Meanwhile many questions remain to be answered. The war was not fought only by members of Parliament nor was it only fought in London; the armies on each side consisted, to a large degree, of pressed men: what did they think the struggle was all about? How, in fact, could the occasion for a split in Parliament become the occasion for an all-embracing civil war? It may be useful in the future to bring to bear on such questions another approach suggested by David Clarke, an archaeologist, who was also faced with the problem of discerning significant groupings in the evidence which has survived – and in the case of archaeology this may well be very little indeed.

Clarke tortuously observed:

> We have become familiar with models as conceptual tools made of structured systems of hypotheses which offer a partially accurate predictive framework for the organization of data. The kinds of model vary from dots and lines to sealing-wax and string or ordered sentences and mathematical expressions. Whatever their material, these structures depend upon the deliberate and arbitrary rejection of some elements of the data whilst retaining other elements which may then be arranged in a specific manner in order to obtain a marked regularity.[55]

He stressed that such a procedure may be wholly artificial: the pattern imposed may be a creation in the mind of the investigator which does not 'belong' to the reality of what is being investigated. But this does not invalidate the procedure, because the purpose is not to prove the existence of a pattern in the original, but by imposing a series of different possibilities to isolate those elements which appear always (or usually) not to fit. This is, in other words, a deliberately *theoretical* strategy, which simply opens up ground for investigation: it is not the investigation itself. It follows that there may be a real importance in looking at the material which does not fit into major and generalized hypotheses.

If we apply this approach to the parties of the Civil War, we would have to move from looking at similarity to looking much more closely at the people who are always singled out as exceptions. It has been stressed that family allegiance played its part in determining the allegiance of individuals, and that members of the family and their tenants held together, but that there were exceptions: the earl of Warwick fought on a different side to his son Robert; even the redoubtable Hampdens had some erring members.[56] Mrs Pearl has drawn attention to the fact that nineteen City aldermen supported the king and five supported Parliament;[57] it might be instructive to look very carefully indeed into those five. Christopher Hill has followed the lead of others in drawing attention to the way in which in any one shire the main contestants for major office took opposite sides in the conflict and, as in Staffordshire, the older families sided with the king and the newer with Parliament;[58] but what of the shires where this did not happen?

It may well be impossible for a student during a short period of historical study, whether directed towards examinations or anything else, to answer all these questions. But he can begin to recognize that they exist, and he can, of course, begin to ask them (and others) for himself. The better he succeeds in doing so, the better he will write; his essays will carry more conviction because they will respond more sensitively to the complex elements in past situations. Chesterton once defined charity as 'a reverent agnosticism about the complexities of the human soul'. Whether or not the historian should be charitable to the past, it is a part of his responsibility to recognize the complexities of human affairs. This does not mean that in his attempt to answer questions posed in historical study, he must be wholly agnostic, but that his judgements cannot, in the nature of the case, become 'a bedrock of accepted fact'. A reverence towards complexity, tempered by imagination and insight, and controlled always by the nature of the evidence, are important attitudes to learn in evaluating the situations in which men found themselves involved many centuries ago and in comprehending the thoughts which determined their actions. Moreover the cultivation of such attitudes is not without importance to those assessing the problems which face us today.

Yet in emphasizing the difficulties, as well as the worthwhile nature, of the subject, we are also recognizing the problems of the reviewer and examiner. It will remain the case that good historians will not always be recognized, since human beings are fallible: first-class historians do not always get first-class degrees, and scholars in every age have frequently not received appropriate appreciation. In historical study, as elsewhere, there are prophets without honour. The failure of the University of Oxford to recognize fittingly, and at the right moment, the talents of Sir Lewis Namier is a reminder that, however gifted a scholar may be, he does not always gain the recognition that is his due.

Notes

1. *A Relation ... of the Island of England*, ed. C. A. Sneyd (Camden Society, 1847), p. 46.
2. C. A. J. Armstrong, 'The Inauguration Ceremonies of the Yorkist kings and their Title to the Throne', *Transactions of the Royal Historical Society*, 30 (1948), pp. 51 ff.
3. J. R. Lander, 'Council, Administration and Councillors 1461–85', *Bulletin of the Institute of Historical Research*, 32 (1959), pp. 138 ff.; *The Anglica Historia of Polydore Vergil* AD 1485–1537, ed. D. Hay (Camden Society, 1950), p. 133.
4. B. P. Wolffe, 'The Management of English Royal Estates under the Yorkist Kings', *English Historical Review*, 71 (1956), pp. 1 ff.
5. F. C. Dietz, *English Government Finance 1485–1558*, 2nd ed.

(1964), p. 51: 'the new financial system *for which the foundations were laid in 1485*' (italics mine).

6. Wolffe, *EHR*, 71, pp. 1 ff.
7. B. P. Wolffe, *The Crown Lands 1461–1536* (1970), p. 66.
8. J. M. W. Bean, *The Decline of English Feudalism 1215–1540* (1968), pp. 235 ff.
9. D. L. Keir, *The Constitutional History of Modern Britain 1485–1951*, 5th ed. revised (1957), p. 6.
10. J. R. Lander, 'Attainder and Forfeiture 1453–1509', *Historical Journal* 4 (1961), pp. 119 ff.; W. H. Dunham, 'Lord Hastings' Indentured Retainers 1461–83', *Transactions of the Connecticut Academy of Arts and Sciences*, 39 (1956–7), pp. 90 ff.
11. G. R. Elton, *The Tudor Revolution in Government* (1959), *passim*.
12. See for example: P. Williams and G. L. Harriss, 'A Revolution in Tudor History?', *Past and Present*, 25 (1963), pp. 3–58; and the debate which ensued in *Past and Present*, 26, 29, 31 and 32.
13. W. A. Morris, *The Medieval English Sheriff to 1300* (1927), pp. 111 ff.
14. The exact nature and extent of these reforms is the subject of scholarly debate. See especially, D. M. Stenton, *English Justice between the Norman Conquest and the Great Charter 1066–1215* (1965), pp. 22 ff.; H. G. Richardson and G. O. Sayles, *The Governance of Medieval England from the Conquest to Magna Carta* (1963), pp. 173 ff.; 438 ff.; J. C. Holt, 'The Assizes of Henry II: the Texts', in *The Study of Medieval Records* (ed. D. A. Bullough and R. L. Storey), pp. 85–106.
15. For a magisterial discussion of these, see J. E. A. Jolliffe, *Angevin Kingship* (1955), *passim;* W. Ullmann, *Principles of Government and Politics in the Middle Ages* (1961), esp. pp. 150 ff.
16. W. Ullmann, *The Growth of Papal Government in the Middle Ages* (1955), *passim*; C. R. Cheney, *From Becket to Langton* (1956), p. 49.
17. Cheney, *From Becket to Langton*, pp. 89 ff.
18. Ibid, p. 90.
19. Ibid, p. 97.
20. C. R. Cheney, *Hubert Walter* (1967), pp. 5–9; J. W. Gray, 'The *Ius Praesentandi* in England from the Constitutions of Clarendon to Bracton', *English Historical Review*, 67 (1952), pp. 481 ff.
21. D. Knowles, *The Historian and Character and Other Essays* (1963), p. 7.
22. D. Knowles, *Thomas Becket* (1970), p. 55.

23. Knowles, *Thomas Becket*, pp. 160–1.
24. W. Camden, *Britannia* (1610), p. 449.
25. F. M Powicke, *Henry III and the Lord Edward* (1947), pp. 84–122.
26. W. Stubbs, *Select Charters* ed. H. W. C. Davies, 9th ed., (1951), p. 288 (cap. 32).
27. Stubbs, *Select Charters*, p. 295 (cap. 14).
28. Ibid, p. 337.
29. For a clear discussion of these questions see E. F. Jacob, *Studies in the Period of Baronial Reform* (1925): B. Wilkinson, *Studies in the Constitutional History of the Thirteenth and Fourteenth Century*, 2nd ed. (1952), and R. F. Treharne, *The Baronial Plan of Reform 1258–1263* (1932).
30. R. F. Treharne, 'The Personal Role of Simon de Montfort in the Period of Baronial Reform and Rebellion 1258–65', *Proceedings of the British Academy*, XI (1954), pp. 75 ff.
31. *The Political Songs of England*, ed. T. Wright (Camden Society, 1839), pp. 72–121.
32. W. Stubbs, *The Constitutional History of England* (1880), II, p. 554.
33. G. T. Lapsley, 'The Parliamentary Title of Henry IV', in *Crown, Community and Parliament in the Later Middle Ages* (1951), pp. 273 ff.
34. B. Wilkinson, 'The Deposition of Richard II and the Accession of Henry IV', reprinted in *Historical Studies of the English Parliament*, ed. E. B Fryde and Edward Miller (1970), I, pp. 329–53. This article also contains excellent further references notably to the work of V. H. Galbraith and M. V. Clarke.
35. Wilkinson, in *Historical Studies of the English Parliament*, p. 353.
36. G. R. Elton, *The Tudor Constitution* (1960), p. 323.
37. See for example C. Williams, *English Historical Documents*, V, (1967), pp. 651 ff.
38. S. E. Lehmberg, *The Reformation Parliament 1529–1536* (1970), pp. 2–7.
39. M. Bowker, *The Secular Clergy in the diocese of Lincoln 1495–1520* (1968); P. Heath, *English Parish Clergy on the Eve of the Reformation* (1969).
40. Some such evidence of reform does exist but it still needs careful research: see especially M. Bowker, 'Lincolnshire 1536: Heresy, Schism or Religious Discontent?', in *Studies in Church History* (1972), IX, ed. D. Baker, pp. 195 ff.
41. A. G. Dickens, *The English Reformation* (1964), p. 116.

42. Bowker, 'Lincolnshire 1536; Heresy, Schism or Religious Discontent', in *Studies in Church History*, IX, p. 195.
43. See E. Jenkins, *Elizabeth and Leicester* (1961). For Miss Jenkins' use of the psychological approach see especially pp. 10 ff.
44. J. E. Neale, *Queen Elizabeth I* (1934; 2nd ed. 1960), p. 74.
45. D. M. Loades, *Two Tudor Conspiracies* (1965), p. 199.
46. Ibid, pp. 245–6.
47. Ibid, pp. 84, 123, 136.
48. Ibid, pp. 78–80.
49. Ibid, p. 86.
50. A statement of the basic theory lying behind this interpretation occurs in K. Marx, *Manifesto of the Communist Party*; for a convenient anthology of further basic texts see especially that edited by Robert Freedman, *Marx on Economics* (London 1961). For a Russian interpretation of the Civil War, see Christopher Hill, *Puritanism and Revolution* (1958, 2nd ed. 1962), p. 6 note 2.
51. D. Brunton and D. H. Pennington, *Members of the Long Parliament* (1954), pp. 15–6, 176 ff.
52. C. Hill, *Puritanism and Revolution*, pp. 19 ff.
53. V. Pearl, *London and the Outbreak of the Puritan Revolution* (1961), pp. 107 ff.; see also C Hill, *Puritanism and Revolution*, pp. 15–17.
54. L. Stone, *The Crisis of the Aristocracy, 1558–1641* (1965) and the subsequent discussion of Professor Stone's conclusions in the *Economic History Review*, 25 (1972), pp. 114 ff.
55. D. L. Clarke, *Analytical Archaeology* (1968, 2nd ed. 1971), p. 441.
56. Mary Keeler, *The Long Parliament 1640–1* (Philadelphia 1954), p. 30.
57. Pearl, *London and the Outbreak of the Puritan Revolution*.
58. Hill, *Puritanism and Revolution*, pp. 22–3.

5 *British History 1700-1945: The Economic Problem and the Approach*

Clive Trebilcock

Modern British history from 1700 poses few simple problems and supplies few simple answers. The documentary evidence is voluminous, but still frequently insufficient to allow of firm conclusions; the possibilities for controversy are infinite. The 'swings', 'cycles' and changes of direction in the broad political, social and economic movements are continuous and rapid. But no area exhibits a variety more pronounced, a documentation more treacherous, a controversy more acute, or a flux more ceaseless than the economic history of the period from 1700 to 1945. Even the most crude analysis of Britain's economic performance over these years could not help but produce an account of startling contrasts and intricately ironic reversals. This chapter, therefore, will concentrate on problems in economic history, although some of the solutions propounded and advice offered will also be relevant to the study of modern social and constitutional history.

The early eighteenth century provided a logical introduction for the economic diversity that was to follow. During its first five or six decades a business community already enjoying great commercial prosperity was occupied in making its preparations for the acquisition of yet greater industrial wealth; the foundations for the world's first industrial economy were gradually laid down. Then, once this process was completed, the economy entered another, more active, stage: it began, after about 1780, to expand at unusual speed, creating an 'industrial revolution' or an 'industrial take-off', or achieving the state of 'critical industrial mass'.[1] Whether the analogies are taken from politics, from aeronautics, or from physics, the historical fact eludes them; but that fact included, nevertheless, an unprecedented acceleration in industrial output between the approximate dates 1780 and 1815. By 1850 this gradual quickening of pace had worked another transformation: the early industrial system had been converted into a far more sophisticated economic organism, endowed with a comprehensive factory style of manufacture, an expanding railroad network, and a secure primacy in world trade.[2] Unfortunately, however, the equilibrium of industrial maturity was not to endure for long. The last third of the nineteenth century brought a further and more radical change of mood: the rate of growth declined, technological leadership was lost, foreign competition intervened, and the puzzled Victorians expressed their dismay by labelling the period between 1873 and 1896 as the 'Great Depression'.[3] It proved to possess characteristics that were slow to desert the economy. Although British exports and British investment recovered in the years before the Great War – indeed to record heights – the prosperity thus generated was flimsily supported; no radical new courses were charted to avoid the foreign threat, no novel technological bases were created. Industry before 1914 went on very much as usual – as long as customers for traditional commodities could be found in increasingly far-flung areas of the world. During the inter-war years, of course, they were scarcely to be found at all, and a final phase of severe economic embarrassment set in. A second Great Depression of far greater ferocity than the first formed the context for the decline of the great staple industries, the appearance of mass unemployment – and the eventual emergence of a compensating force contained within the new industries such as motor-cars, rayon, and electrical goods. But to most outward appearances, the missile which experienced 'take-off' in the late eighteenth century had spent a good part of its momentum after 1918 and was brought to a definitive halt by the Great Crash of 1929–31. Recovery before the Second World War came slowly and was by no means fully consolidated before hostilities commenced.[4] From 1700 through to 1945, then, the British economy exhibits a considerable range of behaviour: it grows organically and decays organically, it rallies and relapses, it grows depressed and emerges resurgent.

How is the student best advised to attempt analysis of this versatile economic monster? How can its moods be accurately gauged? How can the controversies stirred by its apparently contradictory actions be resolved? What is the purpose and legitimacy of the strange language which surrounds it – is it proper for one and the same economic system to 'take-off' like an aeroplane, to 'mature' like a rare wine or a favourite pipe, and to grow 'depressed' like a psychotic? To what extent is this system properly studied by historical methods? – or does the student require knowledge of additional techniques, among them perhaps the skills of the economist, the statistician, or the sociologist? The answers to these questions are not simple, but, then again, the rewards to be achieved from pursuing the answers are not inconsiderable. The student who approaches the monster in a composed and common-sense way, bearing in mind a number of useful runes and incantations, will draw much knowledge and some profit from this field of inquiry.

To begin with, the historian will find that his knowledge of political and social history is extended and deepened by the addition of an economic component. It is, for example, scarcely possible to comprehend the political significance of the 'Church and King' riots of the 1790s, of the 1832 Reform Act, of the 1848 Chartist débâcle, or of the 1911 National Insurance Act without some appreciation of the economic circumstances surrounding them. Naturally enough, industrial change brought modifications in social structure that were in turn to engender massive political and constitutional repercussions. By the 1830s, for instance, a prosperous and distinct business (or middle) class had come into existence; it remained too large for absorption within the traditional propertied groups, yet fully aware of its special political and economic ambitions. It required the 1832 Act and – after energetic propaganda by the Anti-Corn Law League – Peel's inauguration of free trade and repudiation of the Corn Laws in 1846 to serve these interests. Next in line after the solidifying middle classes came a skilled working element, considered by the 1860s sufficiently 'responsible' to deserve the franchise – and duly given it by the Second Reform Act of 1867. In addition, as industrialism extended, a mass labour movement began to grow up, beginning with the 'New Unionism' of the 1880s and speedily developing considerable organizational and political muscles. By the early 1900s it was using these muscles to extract much-needed welfare legislation from the governments of the day. These few examples should demonstrate the impossibility of drawing a solid frontier between economic history and political history in the nineteenth century: plainly, economic change helps to explain political change.

Yet economic history cannot be studied or presented in the same way as constitutional, ecclesiastical or diplomatic history. There are some essential points of difference between it and all other branches of historical investigation. As many note with alarm, the chief of these starts clear out of its pages: they are littered with figures. Necessarily, a form of history which describes economic growth, and does so in alliance – however uneasy or distant – with economic theory, must deal in quantities. But for the student, perhaps educated almost wholly in an arts discipline, the shock of encountering a *numerate* history can be very painful.

Fortunately there are ways of avoiding the 'number phobia' engendered by economic history. The schools themselves, by training increasing numbers of arts students with some mathematical skills or by providing rapidly expanding teaching capacity in both economics and economic history, have assisted enormously. But there is still no real reason why the quite unmathematical arts student should dread the statistical man-traps of economic history and consider them to be impassable hazards. For the most regrettable aspect of the 'number phobia' is that it is a falsely inspired fear. Certainly, it would be pleasant – not least for teachers and lecturers – if all budding economic historians were given an adequate grounding in statistical techniques and economic theory, but very serviceable answers can quite readily be produced without this grounding. The key point is to realize that statistics possess no special life of their own; they are, in the vast majority of cases, illustrative of an argument that can be, and usually is, rendered in other ways. The simplest form of historical statistic, the table or series, is essentially 'narrative', whatever its subject. It recounts a story about the development of industrial output or of foreign trade, for example, and it will do so in a manner meant both to supplement and to summarize – but not to replace – the interpretation which the historian will set alongside it in his text. By the same token, the student may safely employ extracts from these statistical data in *illustration* of his own arguments. Even the more intricate work which economic historians have carried out – on such topics as cyclical movements in industrial output, or cyclical swings in investment or building activity – constitutes an attempt to describe a definite operational rhythm within the economic organism. In such cases the quantitative series have at least the readily understood purpose of *supporting* a well-advertised theoretical contention.

The student should not shy away from these statistical materials. After all, he is not expected to perform prodigies of mathematical ingenuity. Indeed, however desirable it may be, it is not strictly essential that he should fully understand the methodology by which the various tables, indices or series were compiled, any more than it is essential that he should understand the research techniques by which the diplomatic historian works through the original sources to his published reconstruction of events. The teacher will not expect his pupils to provide, in addition to the basic skills in the assessment and deployment of the massive published evidence, the highly advanced skills which, in the first instance, produced the published evidence; all that he may legitimately ask is that the student should approach the results themselves with a critical and creative judgement. Following this course, useful points can certainly be made by examining the statistical item for itself, assessing it as one would any other piece of evidence. Thus, any defects in the data admitted by the author, or revealed by chronological gaps in the series, should not be passed over but carefully examined for their relevance to the stated purpose of the table or index – it is not unknown for such faults to be fatal to the intention of the compiler. The suitability of the time-span and of the time-intervals (decadal? half-decadal? five-year moving averages?) employed should be tested. For instance, does a real wage index begin in a year of famous boom and end in one of notorious slump? If so, something is amiss. Does an unemployment index, by using decadal intervals of sampling, happen to settle on years of unusual cyclical distress? If so, something is amiss. In these ways, and every other way, the 'fit' between the quantitative results and the available qualitative evidence should be most carefully examined. Perhaps most obviously of all, the figures should be studied for any trend, or break in trend, that they may reveal. With surprising frequency the alert student is able to detect his own continuities or turning points, often ones other than those the compiler has chosen to emphasize – and then he is presented with a case of his own to make out. None of these ploys requires startling statistical brilliance, merely common sense applied as coolly to this form of evidence as to any other, and a refusal to be dismayed because the material is presented in an unfamiliar form.

Recently, however, the number problem has been further complicated by the emergence of a group of economists-cum-historians practising a discipline that has been christened the 'new economic history'. As this tool of analysis is increasingly directed towards the British economy of the late nineteenth century and of the inter-war period, its findings are inevitably filtering into the essential reading for these subjects. The basic methodology is quantitative in an entirely novel manner, employing sophisticated statistical techniques in a form of historical probability analysis. The most common device is to construct a 'counter-factual' situation – as with Professor Fogel's famously hypothetical version of the nineteenth-century American economy in which the railroads were *not* built – and then to calculate the difference between the historical actuality and the likely situation as it would have been had some specified variable been radically altered. By this means the contribution of the specified variable – for instance, the contribution of the railroad to the nineteenth-century American economy or of export growth to the British economy over the years 1870–1914 – can be measured. With such techniques, the mathematical procedures are so complex that Professor Mathias has recently been moved to write, 'comprehension is not attainable simply through the application of higher common sense'.[5] For the academic researcher in economic history who needs to comprehend the entire formulation of the case, this is clearly true. But for the undergraduate or pre-university student of economic history who can scarcely be expected to possess in addition the skills of the statistician or econometrician, the 'higher common sense' is precisely the weapon to pit against the 'new economic history'. And it is no mean one. For the student's task is not primarily to judge the mathematical adroitness of the econometrician; it is rather to assess critically the assumptions upon which the calculations are based, the range of the treatment, and the plausibility of the conclusions. Given this brief, there should be no shortage of comment open to the student, for some of the basic contentions put forward by the 'new economic historians' are, at the very least, arguable.

Recent work on the late Victorian economy provides a useful instance. Here, Professor McCloskey has contended that the British industrial system of the period 1870–1900 did not 'fail' but instead performed as well as could be expected given the available resources of capital and labour.[6] In the process, however, he surely leaves it open for the student to point out that the econometrician has assumed, throughout his calculations and arguments, that another important element, the level of technology, may be regarded as a fixed and constant item. There is, indeed, in McCloskey's work the explicit *a priori* supposition, based on no quantitative evidence, nor on evidence of any other kind, that technology is 'international', that it moves, and moved, fluidly and quickly between countries. This is scarcely an argument; rather curiously from a 'new economic historian', it is a simple article of faith, and a very dubious one. In fact British technology in this period lagged considerably behind world 'best practice' technology and there was considerable room for *variation* in the element assumed as fixed by the economic calculation. Despite McCloskey, the late Victorian economy *could* perhaps have improved its technology by following foreign examples, and, if it had done so, its over-all performance could only have been more impressive than it turned out historically. It is thus possible to throw doubt on McCloskey's conclusions – not by sophisticated criticism of his calculations but simply by a common-sense attack upon the assumptions underlying the calculations.

There are a number of similar areas in which the student can score. Any claims by the 'new economic historians' to hold certain elements in their calculations constant, for the sake of mathematical convenience, should be carefully scrutinized. It is entirely possible that the 'fixing' of these elements may be unreal in historical terms, and, unless allowance is made for this, what might have been usefully 'counter-factual' will become a mere flight of fancy. Any attempt to limit the range of the study unreasonably should also be treated with suspicion. Is it permissible, for instance, to test the rationality of the British investment system within a calculation representative *only* of the British capital market, as Professor Edelstein has recently attempted to do? Should not some comparison with the standard provided by the more 'entrepreneurial' banking systems of continental Europe be included if any worthwhile scale of 'rationality' is to be defined?[7] But, perhaps most of all, the student should remain alert for the tactic by which the econometricians tend to relegate important non-quantifiable variables – such as the role of the businessman or entrepreneur – to the status of 'residuals' in their calculations. Problems such as the low productive efficiency of the British coal industry around 1910 are *wholly* explained by the 'new economic historians' in terms of objective measurable factors such as the deepness of the mines and the thinness of the coal seams.[8] By elimination the mine-owner becomes a 'residual'. The argument holds that in the face of the objective difficulties there can be no business 'failure' and the entrepreneur may thus be safely left out of account. This procedure is open to the serious logical objection that the econometric formulation cannot, as yet, encompass anything like the total number of relevant variables – some of these, along with the entrepreneur, will be left out of account, and perhaps less deliberately. Hypothetically, a number of these omitted variables could be *positive* in effect – the quality of British labour, for instance – and thus might partially compensate for the deepness of mines and thinness of seams, implying that these alone could not have explained away the entire one hundred per cent of the productivity problem, and suggesting that entrepreneurial conservatism, among other factors, should be introduced into the explanation.

Given careful thought along lines such as these, there is no reason why the student should not make effective points even in the most ostensibly quantitative areas of economic history. However, it would certainly not be appropriate if his attitude to the 'new economic history' were to become uniformly destructive. The discipline is a young one and will, no doubt, grow increasingly sophisticated with time. In its present state of development, it should be viewed critically, yet not dismissed lightly. Careful marksmanship may shoot down parts of it, but it deserves better than the undiscriminating volley from the over-eager opponent. Allowing this qualification, it could certainly be contended that, within the undergraduate or pre-university essay topic touched by the 'new economic history', calmly directed logic can be no less effective as an analytical tool than statistical training. In the final instance, as Professor Mathias has concluded, 'the historian's critical standards will remain the test of these hypotheses'.[9]

The student of economic history does not have only to contend with quantitative problems, however. He must also deal with the explanatory 'models' frequently employed by economic historians.[10] Generally speaking, a 'model' is an abstract construction of ideal circumstances or essential characteristics which can be used to *represent* large-scale phenomena such as 'industrialization' or the 'international monetary system'. It is not essential – nor is it possible – that the model should describe exactly the industrial experience or the monetary policy of any particular country or historical situation; its utility is rather that the historical actuality for any given case may be measured against the ideal or quintessential standard provided by the model. Thus, in one especially well-known example, Professor Rostow has chosen to depict the process of industrial development in a simple multi-stage system.[11] In the terms of his model the archetypal economy will pass from apprenticeship to mature proficiency through a series of well-defined phases.

The initial phase, from which the expanding economy must emerge, is that of the 'traditional society', a benighted world 'based on pre-Newtonian science and technology'.[12] If everything goes well, this stage is followed by an era of 'preconditions', a period of preparation during which the agricultural sector will make surpluses of foodstuffs, capital, and manpower available for industrial use, transport and banking facilities will grow more sophisticated, and daring businessmen will emerge to direct the new economic course. After these preliminaries will come the stage of 'take-off', a brisk burst of modernization compressed into the span of two or three decades, and characterized by a doubling in the rate of productive investment and the growth of certain strategic industries to form 'leading sectors' within the economy. From this point irreversible industrialization will set in and the manufacturing sector will assume the state of 'self-sustained growth' – in which development leads on inexorably to further development – and embark upon a fresh stage labelled the 'drive to maturity'. At an advanced moment in this process, a prosperous, technologically progressive and fully-balanced economic system – 'the mature economy' – will be created. In the final stage, it remains only for the industrial institutions of the mature economy to broaden their social range and to transform the entire populace into a single consumer market. When this has been achieved, the 'era of high mass consumption', the *terminus ad quem* of the model, will have been reached. Clearly, in the most general terms, a number of industrial countries could present an economic experience which would at least resemble the morphology of the Rostow 'model'. The British example itself could be used to demonstrate the existence of a 'preconditions' phase covering virtually the first three-quarters of the eighteenth century, the intrusion of a marked acceleration in industrial output (perhaps a 'take-off') in the two decades or so after 1780, the maintenance of steady, sustained growth in the first half of the nineteenth century, the achievement of maturity around 1850–70, and the arrival of 'high mass consumption' during the inter-war years 1919–39.

'Models' like this should hold few terrors for the student. If it is true that the economic historian tends to make unusually frequent use of the 'model' technique, this is probably because of his proximity to the field of economic theory, for all economic statements must involve expectations about the way in which an *ideal* economy – implicitly a species of normative 'model' economy – would react under certain circumstances. But it should be stressed that the economic historian is acting in a manner scarcely different from that adopted by many other breeds of historian. It is perfectly possible for political historians to construct models of 'revolution' or 'nationalism', and some of them do so. In like manner, the student of modern British social or constitutional history is liable to encounter the use of 'models' – perhaps of social structure or of voting behaviour – in these fields, and will face very similar problems in assessing them. On another level, it is surely the case that every student of history will try, whether explicitly or not, to measure a particular industrialization experience, or, for that matter, a particular instance of political revolution, against a notional ideal type. The brain itself, as the biologists now tell us, 'functions by fitting inputs against models'.[13] In his wide-ranging use of measurement by model, therefore, the economic historian is merely stating his assumptions, defining his standards of measurement, somewhat more explicitly than is usual in other fields of historical inquiry or general human endeavour.

Once the student has familiarized himself with the technique of 'modular' analysis he may turn to constructive criticism. This is a form of criticism that is not restricted to the appraisal of 'models' in economic history; social or political 'models' might be assessed in the same style. Since all 'models' set out to resemble as many individual instances as possible – though the identification need not be exact – they are immensely vulnerable: in the event, they may resemble too few instances and diverge from too many. When employing a 'model', the serious scholar must, as Professor Gerschenkron has observed, 'try to discover the limits of its applicability and will be ready to discard it when those limits have been ascertained'.[14] But many scholars find this easier said than done, and grow deeply attached to their creations. With the Rostow model, for instance, it is the case that the precise, compressed spurt of the 'take-off' can be identified in very few historical instances; and yet Professor Rostow has not seen fit to discard it. In Britain itself the doubling in the rate of 'productive investment' from below five per cent to above ten per cent of the national income, a necessary characteristic of 'take-off', appears to have required a much more extended period – not two decades but closer to a century – than that allocated to it by the builder of the 'model'. In many other countries a similar 'stretching' of the 'take-off' phase is increasingly indicated by the data.

The critical student should, therefore, probe at the weak point, carefully test the 'model's' range and discover how often it diverges from the historical record. Furthermore, the degree of over-all compatibility between the mechanisms which the 'model' needs to function and the historical context in which it needs to be set should be fully studied. For instance, the requirements of Rostow's 'preconditions' stage, essential for the build-up of power before take-off – and including, *inter alia*, a 'transforming' agriculture, an emerging transport system and an advancing financial system – have seemed to many observers implausibly sophisticated as characteristics of a *pre*-industrial economy. This point leads on, also, to another method of assessment. With any 'model' which involves a stage system – as many economic, but not only economic, 'models' do – the student should pay special attention to the divisions between the stages: all too often the provision for moving the 'model' from one stage to another is perilously weak. Again, taking the Rostow example, the mechanism for picking the economy out of the 'preconditions' phase and hurling it into the trajectory of 'take-off' remains extremely ill-defined. If methods of analysis such as these are employed, the historian should be able to decide whether the model under scrutiny combines descriptive accuracy with internal consistency in the proper measure – or whether it should be abandoned as an artificial abstraction devoid of historical relevance. Economic, political, and social models alike should yield useful points under this form of assessment.

Perhaps, after this discussion of the tendency to employ analytical models in this subject, it is natural to emphasize that economic history is, before anything else, a research-oriented discipline. In some senses – as with the accelerating quest for statistical precision – this orientation may cause problems for the student, although these are by no means insurmountable. In another sense, however, it is surely the strong element of research activity which gives the subject its compensating attractiveness. For there are considerable advantages in working an expanding frontier. A swift turnover of ideas, a pervasive sense of novelty and discovery, a ready supply of lively discussion, are among the attributes of a subject which turns its face squarely towards research. Moreover, economic history is a subject of problems: the identification, definition, and analysis of problems is virtually the economic historian's stock-in-trade. This is a feature which not only provokes more analytical discussion than simple narrative presentation, but also allows a definite sense of progression as the major questions are recognized, fully described, and, occasionally, resolved.

In order to capitalize upon the most attractive aspects of the subject, the student should keep a weather eye upon the current state of research. This is best achieved by a thorough scrutiny of the specialist journals, particularly the *Economic History Review* or the *Journal of Economic History*. With some important topics, such as the debate over working-class living standards in the period 1750–1850, or the analysis of the demographic explosion after 1740, it is virtually impossible to obtain a full appreciation of the vital issues without reference to the journals. In some ways, though, the increasing availability of collected readings or assortments of papers, published in book form and graced with an introductory summary by an expert editor, has qualified the importance of the learned periodicals for the serious student. But these collections inevitably create a fixed juxtaposition of views, which will be further solidified by the pattern of interpretation suggested by the editor. The result is likely to be that the student will accept the preconceived framework which he is offered and will merely fit the various papers into a ready-made relationship. All too often, he will not develop his own synthesis of the available views and will reproduce, instead, an instantly recognizable proprietary product. This habit, mistaking a clear historical trademark for the latest word on the subject, should be strenuously avoided, and the essayist interested in producing work of any quality would be well advised to cull his own prizes from the journals. Nor is this a recommendation restricted to the undergraduate population: the A-level answers of recent years have revealed that the best pupils and teachers have made use of journals like the *Economis History Review* to considerable effect. British economic history is one historical field in which high-quality research findings are easily available to the student without intermediaries or filters. It is an advantage, of course, which is not unique to economic history although it is especially well-developed in this area: other sectors of modern British history are served by periodicals such as the *Journal of Modern History*, the *English Historical Review*, and *Past and Present*, and the injunction to keep abreast of the current research is one which has a general application across all sectors. Of course the student should be aware that in some fields of history there are very real dangers in chasing the most recent idea simply for its novelty,[15] but he should also realize that the economic branch once again forms something of a special case. Some important topics in modern British economic history are scarcely touched upon outside the journals, and, in a subject currently so reliant upon its researchers for material, the best view of many other topics is often to be gained from the periodicals.

However, the special dependence of economic history upon research sometimes produces strange and unfortunate effects among its disciples. These are avoidable, once they are recognized. It is noteworthy, for instance, that, although the subject is one of many statistics, by no means all of them command outright confidence. Many, such as the eighteenth-century population statistics or the early nineteenth-century real wage indices, are notoriously unreliable. If, in some subjects, the student must take great care to distinguish between the wood and the trees, he must be especially careful in the field of economic history, for there the trees are in a state of constant motion. Research, in this context, consists of an interminable groping for an extra degree of certainty. These deficiencies have been known to reduce students to impotent outrage and their arguments to admissions of inrushing ignorance – if the statistics cannot be trusted, they complain, how is it possible to assert *anything*. This kind of reaction must be avoided. It must be accepted that, in a research subject, the ground in some areas will necessarily be unstable and the possible hypotheses tentative. But this is no reason for refusing to make the best possible use of what materials we have. Not despair with the state of present results, but a willingness to employ what is to hand as flexibly and enterprisingly as possible: this is the mark of the first class answer. It is to the *advantages* conferred by the innovational nature of the subject – the chance of producing a useful insight of one's own, the possibility of linking together a number of research findings in a satisfyingly novel manner – that the student should look.

If doubtful statistics cause dismay, agitation over the basic method of approach is no less frequent. Every teacher is familiar with the essay which agonizes at such length over its analytical framework that little or no attention can be spared for what was to be analysed. Economic history is particularly prone to this fault: the fact that much of the literature is concerned with the communication of research results inevitably means that it is sprinkled with cautious qualifications and rigorous discussions of *modi operandi*. These are frequently – painfully frequently – extracted by the student and built up into an edifice of imposing quasi-sophistication, decorated with borrowed frills, foibles and fears. It is easily done and conveys, with the minimum of effort, an illusion of scholarship. Again it is not restricted to economic history: many other areas of modern British history in which research is active offer very similar temptations to the student. The first class answer, however, should avoid the trick at all costs and in all situations. For it is the trick of creating an overture for which there is no symphony, an infrastructure for which there is no superstructure. A decent space, perhaps a moderately long paragraph, devoted to the methodological introduction, and then a full confrontation of the essay's central proposition remains the best course. The extended consideration of investigative methods should be left where it belongs – in the learned journals.

The close dependence of economic history on research produces a perpetually shifting system of interpretation, a persistent sharpening of distinctions, an occasional lurch in basic assumptions. In this way, in its sensitivity to the need for endless interpretation and re-interpretation, the subject is very much a live one. It is almost a necessary characteristic of the articles in the learned journals that they should carry in their titles the words 'A Revision' or 'A Re-appraisal'. If economic history is a discipline of problems, economic historians seem extremely loath to let the problems rest. The result is a subject of cycles, long cyclical swings in the more basic orthodoxies, faster, more frenetic cycles of controversy. How is the first-class answer to deal with these problems?

To begin with, the insecurity introduced by the bouts of re-interpretation must once more be recognized and accepted as the counterpart to the subject's fertility in ideas. Even the limited certainties offered by other branches of historical inquiry can rarely be duplicated here. It is, therefore, especially important that the student of economic history should remove from his mind the objective of a fixed and definite 'historical truth' and replace it with the goal of the most intellectually satisfying and most fully *credible* interpretation. With the larger cycles of revisionism this is a reasonably simple task, since these 'long swings' appear to be related to movements in the collective consciousness of the discipline and are agreed by the great majority of its practitioners. A good example of such a process might be the unanimity with which the 'cataclysmic' or 'discontinuous' interpretation of economic change has been repudiated in recent years. The concept of industrial and agricultural 'revolutions' has been analysed in detail and found wanting. Theories which emphasize the gradual and accumulative nature of modernization in agriculture and industry have replaced theories stressing the rapidity and violence of economic development. Thus Professors Chambers and Mingay have removed the Agricultural Revolution from where it was left by Lord Ernle, compactly situated in the second half of the eighteenth century, and stretched it in two directions, backwards to the mid-seventeenth century, and forward to the later nineteenth century.[16] Similarly the idea of an industrialization phenomenon which fell upon the economy as suddenly as the Parisian mob upon the Bastille or rose from the economy as abruptly as a missile in 'take-off', has been reworked by many scholars, notably Professors Coleman, Kuznets, Habakkuk and Miss Deane.[17] In the process, as the statistical assessments for trade figures or rates of investment have earned close attention, an interpretation presenting the line of industrial activity as a smooth curve, growing definitely steeper towards the end of the eighteenth century, but exhibiting no marked 'break' in its climb, has gained much ground. Assessments of British industrial growth involving 'discontinuities' or 'turning-points' – as do both 'take-off' and 'revolution' – have suffered by the comparison. The student is thus left with a long-term, gradual upswing of industrial activity within which the 'benchmarks', 'kinks' or 'turning-points' are seen as proportionately much less important than the over-all trend. This version of events has real advantages over the cataclysmic interpretation. For one thing it allows *earlier* spurts of industrial activity, such as Professor Nef's inaptly christened 'Industrial Revolution' of the period 1540–1640, to be placed in a logical relationship with the heightened economic activity of the late eighteenth century, a relationship implying that Nef's 'revolution' (really an industrialization within a single manufacturing sub-sector) occupies an earlier and lower arc of the same curve or series of curves. For another, this revisionist tendency within economic history fits well with a general intellectual characteristic which has been exercising considerable influence over the wide field of historical studies for some time: a distrust of any interpretation featuring the sudden dramatic event, the 'historical thunderbolt', together with a suspicion that all major changes require careful preparation, possess precedents, and result from a gradual accumulation of forces. On yet another level, an interpretation which views the industrial society as gradually created seems *a priori* more compelling than one which presents it as the result of a twenty- or thirty-year storming campaign.

Assimilation of such broad changes in the basic fashions of the subject should not cause the student much hardship. Precisely because they are broad, because they are influenced by the ground-swell that is generated within a discipline by the summation of its research findings, as well as by the more pervasive intellectual currents of the era, these 'long cycles' are usually accepted with little objection. All that is necessary is that the propositions they contain should not be taken to constitute an invariable norm. That a gradualistic interpretation of British industrial growth in the eighteenth and nineteenth centuries appears eminently reasonable does not argue, and should not be taken to argue, that *all* economic change is inherently gradual. There are no inflexible laws of continuity in economic development. British experience, and the experience of some other relatively advanced nations, has demonstrated simply that large industrial changes *need not* emerge from the economy with explosive speed and violence. But in a different context – within the context, let us say, of a backward country able to imitate the industrial achievements of its predecessors and to purchase advanced equipment in ready-made form – there is no reason to suppose that industrial growth should be as gradual as it was for the pioneer manufacturing economies.

Much more disturbing to the average student than the 'long cycles' of high fashion are the 'short cycles' of low controversy. An appreciable number among the most important topics in modern British economic history – the 'standard of living of the workers' between 1750 and 1850; the causation of population growth in the eighteenth century; the degree of connection between imperial interest and trade expansion in the nineteenth century; the measure of retardation in British economic performance after 1870; the 'true' severity of the inter-war depression, have formed the subjects of fierce academic debate within the last two decades. For the student, this particular characteristic of research-oriented scholarship can prove baffling. Which side is right? How is one to choose between the contradictory views presented with equal authority by two embattled historians of obvious eminence? Caught in the cross-fire, the student often develops severe doubts as to his own fitness to judge between Red Force and Blue Force, Northland and Southland. This is a problem which is repeated over large areas of modern British history where research is active. Once more, economic history by presenting its own particularly sharply defined version of the problem makes a point of general relevance.

How then is the first class answer to intrude itself into the dangerous area between the two camps? The first point, not unnaturally, is that usually the position for it is somewhere *between* the two camps, for, in a subject which advances by debate and controversy, it is exceedingly rare for one group to possess a monopoly of the appropriate arguments. Very little is achieved by the essayist who throws in his lot with one side and commits himself wholeheartedly to its arguments: mere imitation, a simple regurgitation of a well-known case, will be the most obvious result. The impassioned tone of one advocate will be provided with an echo, not an analyst. This cannot advance the cause of debate, of scholarship, or of the student. If the process of dialectical confrontation between two protagonists is to be at all fruitful for the student, he must attempt to produce his own synthesis and to cut a path between the two opposing views. The most effective way to achieve this middle position is, above all, to reduce the scale of the controversy; few are as wide-ranging as they may appear. Quite often the conflict is maintained by what amounts to a semantic conspiracy between the two sides, allowing each to take up a more adamant and absolutist position than is in fact necessary. Thus, those who argue that the population growth of the years after 1740 must be explained in terms of a rising birth-rate would appear to be irreconcilably opposed to those who hold that the demographic spurt must be ascribed to a falling death rate – until it is realized that the former school, or at least its main representatives, believe only that the birth-rate exerts the major influence *after a period of high mortality,* or, put differently, when the death-rate has fallen.[18] In this case, it would be quite fair to attribute the population growth to a *combination* of falling death-rate and high birth-rate. A similar difficulty has arisen over the 'Great Depression' of the years 1873–96: the semantic impact of this insidious phrase has caused much damage, encouraging one school to search for a 'real' depression with high rates of short-term unemployment, declining rates of export growth, and increasing foreign competition; while, in reaction, another body of opinion dismisses the 'reality' of depression, minimizes the long-term unemployment rate, and points to rising absolute levels of exports, industrial output and national wealth.[19] Here, both sides could well be brought to agreement in the concept of 'retardation': if the economy was not in absolute terms depressed, it was certainly, in growth terms, decelerating, and it would be a rash controversialist indeed, whether of the 'new' or 'old' species of economic historian, who disagreed with this trimming statement.

Another method of out-manoeuvring controversy is contained in the injunction *'regardez la chronologie'*. Academic disputes frequently choose for themselves the wide canvas, the sweep of a contested century, yet there is often a substantial amount of concealed agreement between the disputants over a major part of the period: what is heralded as a full-scale battle fought over an extended front can often be reduced to a limited skirmish with one or two decades as its tactical objective.

There is, too, the question of data, and its selection. If one historian produces his effect by choosing certain data from specified years, and another achieves an opposite effect by taking different data from a second set of years, then the student is issued with an automatic invitation to scrutinize the compatibility of the different blocks of information, and the comparability of the years taken as samples. It can often be demonstrated that the different sets of data are not fully consistent one with another, or, even more frequently, that special and opposed characteristics attach to the years chosen by the two sides to support their contending claims.

The purpose of narrowing the controversy is not to create an agreed central position, purged of interest and energetic commitment, but to forestall crude and overheated imitation of familiar arguments on the one hand and on the other, to prevent the helpless indecision which many students experience when faced with a hotly disputed issue. More ingenuity is required in finding the common elements, in identifying the over-elaborate defences of artificial controversy, in dovetailing opposed hypotheses, than is ever displayed in the imitative outpourings of the over-committed or the deadly balance-sheets of those who record but cannot decide. Further, there is the question of emphasis or degree. The first class answers does not have to aim for the exact centre. After it has exercised its ingenuity on the fullest possible integration of thesis and antithesis, it is wholly at liberty to tip the balance one way or the other, to opt for a final position of qualified optimism or qualified pessimism. But in either case it ought to show the fullest possible understanding of the cross-currents and complex intercutting of the controversy.

A number of these points may perhaps be rendered more precisely if a single controversy can be examined in detail. Perhaps the most famous, and probably the most hard-fought, duel in recent years took placc between Professor Hobsbawm and Dr Hartwell and concerned the living standards of the British working class in the period 1750–1850. That this bout formed a continuation of an historic contest stretching back on the 'pessimistic' side through the Hammonds, the Webbs and Toynbee to Engels and Marx, and, on the 'optimistic' side, through Clapham and Giffen to Tooke and McCulloch, in no way lessened its heat. Taken up in the *Economic History Review* in 1957, with Professor Hobsbawm wearing the traditional mantle of the pessimist and Dr Hartwell assuming, shortly after, the slightly more unusual costume of the optimist, the combat ran through a number of learned papers, and, thence into hard covers, but with little resolution of the disputed issues.[20] The topic was one which brought in a huge variety of qualifications at the very start. Just what composed the 'standard of living', and how was it determined? If it should be quantitatively measured by real wage indices, unemployment figures, and consumption indicators, was not something left over? Did that something reside in the qualitative aspect of life – the brutality, routine, and impersonality of factory work – and, if so, how could either improvement or deterioration in this area be established? Anyway, were not the statistics for the quantitative measurements almost entirely unreliable? Who were the 'working class'? – artisans? industrial operatives? agricultural workers? And was it not unreal to study them, whoever they were, on a national basis when clearly there were massive regional variations in fortune? Should they not be studied by trade, by locality, even by age group? Many students faced with this battery of doubts and queries either give up all hope of grasping the 'real' topic or discuss the doubts and queries at great length in careful avoidance of the central issue. The truth, of course, is that the statistics are difficult, the qualitative aspect barely manageable, and the regional and occupational information inadequate. What, then, can be achieved with what we have?

To begin with, it is clear that the student is not required to deal with *large* shifts in living standards over the period which is most discussed, that is the years between 1790 and 1840. The 'optimist' is quite willing to admit that economic change affected some groups of workers adversely and is increasingly tending to argue that the falling prices, more regular employment, and wider range of job opportunities of the years after 1815 brought about, for most workers, only a fairly modest improvement in their standard of living. The pessimist, for his part, chooses less frequently to argue that industrialization produced an absolute decline in living standards and now rather emphasizes that the advance which it effected was insufficiently rapid, poorly distributed, and did nothing for the *quality* of life. Thus, Professor Hobsbawm's most recent opinions are curiously lacking in power: 'There was,' he writes, 'quite certainly no significant *general* improvement. There may, *or may not,* have been deterioration between the middle 1790s and the middle 1840s. Thereafter, there was undoubted improvement.'[21] If these are the most definite pessimistic statements now available, it would seem (as so often) that less ground separates the two camps than their rhetoric would suggest – although consensus is still distant.

If examination of the semantics of controversy can reduce its heat, so too can a scrutiny of the chronology. There is, for instance, virtually complete agreement that the period between 1750 and 1790 saw a general if gentle rise in living standards with advancing real wages, improving consumption, and decreasing slackness in the employment market. Again, the inflation and dietary decline of the Napoleonic War period is contested by no one, and no more is the full employment which war brought as a countervailing force. These years would be generally agreed as a phase of deteriorating living standards, or, at best, if a heavy weighting is allowed to the expansion of employment, an era in which the earlier improvement was brought to a halt and a plateau substituted for the preceding upward slope. The five or six years which followed the Vienna Settlement likewise allow of no debate: slashing cuts in government spending, an abrupt falling off in war orders, overcapacity in industry, and a rapid demobilization of troops created a flabby and deflationary economy, a high level of unemployment, and a strident overtone of social unrest. After 1842, when the beginnings of the mid-Victorian boom launched every living standard indicator into a steep ascent, certainty of a different kind is possible. Out of the century of dispute, therefore, a mere two decades or so, the years between 1820 and 1842, are left as the area where conflict is truly intense. On either side of these decades, although the difficult regional and occupational variations remain, and the need for greater statistical precision persists, the broad trends can be indicated with a certain circumscribed assurance.

Within the battle area, however, there is an acute data problem, the information relating to consumption, unemployment, and real wages having provided the ground for endless contention. The consumption evidence in particular has provided a ready source of ammunition for the pessimists. Professor Hobsbawm has argued, for example, that between 1800 and 1840 the supply of some important foodstuffs – and, employing the figures for animals slaughtered at Smithfield Market, he points especially to meat – expanded less rapidly than did the total number of consumers. The basis for this argument is by no means solid, however. If the assessments for the most important commodity, the Smithfield returns for meat, are closely examined, a number of serious deficiencies emerge. The lists of animals slaughtered omit any sufficient allowance for carcase weights, for imported Irish and Scottish cattle, and, most important, for pig products, traditionally the source of the cheapest meat. In addition, other London meat-markets were expanding at this time far more rapidly than Smithfield. As a result, it is difficult to believe that the returns from this single food outlet were representative even of meat consumption in the capital, quite apart from that of the nation as a whole. Assessments for tea, sugar, and tobacco consumption, derived from import returns, are scarcely more helpful since fluctuations in these commodities could as easily reflect changes in taste as in prosperity. At first sight a more hopeful direction seems to have been taken by recent research which has aimed at establishing an aggregate figure for annual consumption per head of population. The resulting tables indicate an upward break in trend between 1811 and 1821 and a sustained rise from 1821 onwards.[22] Unfortunately, however, these statistics can tell us nothing as to how the increase was distributed among the various layers of the population. A critical assessment of the consumption data provides no clear conclusion. All that may be said with certainty is that the pessimistic case – on this point the most energetically promoted – remains unproven.

The unemployment problem is measured no more easily. True, the disputed period was one in which the trade cycle moved with some violence. The pessimists are able to claim that 'the period 1811–42 saw . . . abnormal unemployment',[23] citing examples of acute labour surplus in a number of localities. But these illustrations would succumb to any test which assessed the suitability of their sample years: the great majority are drawn from slump periods and particularly from the troughs of 1826–7 and 1839–42. That unemployment *was* chronic in these years is beyond dispute, but it is also highly significant that prosperity for the labouring groups came and went with great rapidity throughout this phase of the cycle. To extrapolate from the experience of the trough years to a long-term level of 'abnormal' unemployment would seem quite unsuitable in such a context. Moreover, the wage and price data for the period, unreliable though they are, provide certain general indications as to the likelihood of an enduring over-supply of labour. It is common ground that a considerable fall in the general price level took place between 1815 and 1850, and, all things being equal, one might expect – in the absence of effective trade union organizations – that a corresponding downward pressure would be exerted on the price of labour. If there had been also a persistent surplus of workers in the market, then a second downward force – provided by the superabundance of labourers bidding for jobs – would have pressed upon the wage-rate. The price of labour would thus come under a powerful double attack. But, in the event, although the deflationary pressure was indisputably present, the level of wage rates in money terms remained remarkably *stable* throughout the period. The inference would appear to be that the hypothetical labour surplus (i.e. unemployment), the second downward force, could not have existed for any extended period. Otherwise, the variations in wage-rates would surely have been more violent than the very modest ones on the record. The unemployment issue, therefore, provides useful examples of the dangers involved in deriving trends from information sampled in untypical years. It also indicates that, although no precise quantitative gauge of unemployment is available, and the regional variations remain unpredictable, the delineation of certain probabilities should not lie outside the reach of the student.

A third danger area, the minefield formed by the real wage evidence, remains to be crossed. Here the lack of specific regional or occupational material is very marked and – with the exception of valuable series recently produced for the cities of Bath and Glasgow[24] – real wage figures have often to be compiled by a very dangerous procedure, applying *London* price evidence to wage information from many other areas. However, it is again possible to establish a few likelihoods. It is noticeable, for instance, that the wage calculations carried out by Perkin using three *separate* sources of price information result in three distinct real wage indices which, nevertheless, behave in a very *similar* fashion.[25] Each shows a substantial rise 1810–24, each a modest fall 1824–40, each a definite rise 1840–5. The correspondence between several indices, compiled by different methods, and based on materials much criticized for their haphazardness and selectivity is, at least, interesting. If this type of wage information *is* taken at face value some useful emphases are possible. That the data indicate a fall in real wages during the 1830s has permitted an important pessimistic argument to revolve around a probable loss in the workers' purchasing power over these years. Yet, it is, once more, necessary to relate this contention specifically to its context. This would reveal that the decline occurred from a level higher than any achieved since 1780, was modest in scale, and was reversed immediately after the deep cyclical downswing of 1839–42. If the information is *not* taken at face value, one of the most important criticisms to be made would involve the admission that it is likely to understate rather than overstate any improvement in purchasing power. This is so because the available price data for the period include a restricted sample of *manufactured* commodity prices. Now, during an era of increasing industrial output and efficiency, these prices would be likely to move downwards faster than the average. So, any index which contained too few of them would be bound to *under*-represent the over-all price fall and the improvement in purchasing power. These observations should make it possible to accept, on the one hand, a limited slide in real wages during the 1830s but to postulate, on the other, a moderate but definite upward trend over the period 1820–45. Exactly how these gains were distributed by region and trade is a subject requiring – and gradually receiving – more research.

Finally there is the problem of the qualitative standard, the 'quality of life' rather than the 'standard of living'. Here the difficulties would be much eased by an acceptance of the proposition that all welfare indicators need by no means move in the same direction. It is perfectly possible for a man to be more consistently employed, more regularly fed, and to be earning more in real terms while the urban environment in which he works and lives steadily deteriorates. No optimist would be well advised to contest this, nor to minimize the squalor and disease which resulted as the Victorian towns succumbed to over-population and crumbled into disrepair.[26] Again the student's task is to put the problem into context. In fact, slum conditions were as much a blight upon the *non*-industrial towns of the period, cities such as Edinburgh or Exeter, as upon the great centres of manufacturing. Not too much industry but too many people created urban deterioration; it was as much a demographic as an economic effect. Similarly, the contention that slum conditions represented a deterioration in environment by any pre-industrial standard is a considerable oversimplification: the broken-down villages of the early eighteenth century, the 'rural slums', provide proof that the pre-industrial countryside harboured its own scandals. It is indeed generally important to challenge the thesis that industrialization necessarily brought a ruinous change in the quality of life, to emphasize that the 'horrors of the factory system' possessed a considerable if disreputable pedigree. Deficiencies in the 'quality of life' existed well before 1750 and they were not confined to slum conditions in the countryside. If factory life led to 'alienation' and 'depersonalization' of work relationships, to deterioration in the bond between master and man, it could scarcely have introduced relationships more remote than those which commonly existed, under the traditional régime of the domestic outworking system, between the travelling merchant-entrepreneur and the isolated cottage worker. Again, if the great industrial towns are charged with the twin evils of unemployment and disease, the pre-industrial countryside must face similar allegations – involving heavy seasonal unemployment and underemployment, periodic crop failures, and the epidemics which frequently followed the harvest losses. The point is not that a comparison can be made between the quality of pre-industrial life and the quality of factory life; the two social and economic systems were so distinct as to forbid any effective juxtaposition. It is rather that all judgements as to whether the industrial system was 'better' or 'worse' than what preceded it are better avoided. The frequently encountered view that industrialization involved the sacrifice of some rare bucolic utopia on the altar of Mammon should be abandoned. A more sensible conclusion might be that the 'quality of life' for agricultural labourers before 1750 and for industrial workers after 1750 was roughly constant in its unpleasantness.

Furthermore, the idea that industrial change brought *abrupt* changes in the 'quality of life' requires extensive modification. The 'satanic mill' of industrialism did not suddenly spring up to dominate economy and skyline with its dark barracks and malodorous chimneys; the factory did not become the characteristic unit of industrial organization before the 1830s or 1840s. Until then, the more usual context for industrial labour was the workshop, the small work-group, within which the strains of depersonalization and occupational monotony would be much less severe than those associated with factory life. In other words, the adjustment of the work-force to the new systems of manufacturing was gradual and the major part of this adjustment came at a time when more tangible gains in the standard of living were either within reach, or very nearly so.

What synthesis emerges from this discussion? Neither the pessimist nor the optimist case in regard to consumption patterns for the period 1820–42 can be said to possess much force. Unemployment in some years was undoubtedly severe, as the pessimists allege, but appears unlikely as a long-term problem, as the optimists rightly point out. Real wages did follow a moderately 'pessimistic' course in the 1830s, but this was insufficient to divert them from a generally 'optimistic' upward trend 1820–45. As for the 'quality of life', the pessimist can point with conviction to very real problems of urban decay, while the optimist can stress the squalor of *pre*-industrial life and the *gradual* spread of the factory system. This integration of the two opposing blocks of material can be strengthened by a simple analysis of the cyclical swings over the disputed decades. Since the cycle operated with considerable force, it is not difficult to identify the 'bad' years – 1826–7, 1830–1, 1839–42 – and the 'good' ones – 1821–6 and 1832–6. It quickly becomes obvious that much of the data employed by the pessimists is drawn from the 'bad' years and much of that used by the optimists from the 'good' years. This should suggest a solution. The slant of the employment and real wage data would suggest a restrained upward trend over the period as a whole. However, the pessimists must be allowed due credit for the 'bad' years, for the periodically critical levels of unemployment and for the deeply unsatisfactory state of the industrial towns. A modest upward movement in living standards marred by sporadic crises of considerable severity would seem to be the most satisfactory answer; it allows a good deal to either side.

As an important incidental it is useful to recall for this period the connection between economic and political events and to relate the living standards evidence to its political and social context. It was, in this sense, no accident that the post-war depression after 1815 witnessed violent protest in towns as far apart as Falmouth and Carlisle as well as the more spectacular events provided by the final depredations of the Luddites, the march of the 'Blanketeers' and the unfortunate incident at St Peter's Field, Manchester when a political reform meeting was ridden down by the local yeomanry.[27] Similarly, the unstable period 1820–45 raises interesting questions, since it contained a major movement for electoral reform, the campaigns of the middle-class Anti-Corn Law League for the abolition of protection, and the threatening activities of the Chartists. Certainly, the fortunes of the Chartist leadership relied heavily on the swing of the business cycle for its support, attracting an important following only in years of economic dislocation such as 1839–42, and losing ground catastrophically as economic conditions improved, as they did in the 1840s. Conversely, the emergent trade union movement took over the case for the working man in the upswing of the cycle and presented it in an altogether less violent style. But, even here, economic crisis had the power to radicalize the unions, bringing the concept of the 'general trades union' and the 'general strike' to the forefront after 1829. As the middle class gained in prosperity – but within a disturbed social framework which kept governments extremely sensitive to all forms of agitation – and as working-class fortunes waxed and waned, significant political consequences necessarily followed.

From this discussion of the living standards issue should emerge by contrast a reasonably clear picture of the answer that is best avoided. This answer would list the doubts, reservations and uncertainties of the debate at great length. It would be dismayed by the tentative state of the statistics and would resort to general remarks about the woeful state of ignorance which these reveal. It would be puzzled by the disagreements between the various schools of interpretation, and, in consequence, would catalogue the views of the opposing sides, while refraining from attempting either a reconciliation or a general conclusion. It would fail to perceive that, in some areas, the disagreement is much less marked than would at first appear. The student interested in high quality answers should note these hazards and avoid them. He should also realize that useful results can be achieved by the careful handling of even partial or flawed statistics. He should learn to aim for the centre of controversy, mapping and setting down the areas of broad agreement as he passes. He should recognize that the controversialists will often manipulate the debate by the selection of time-frames suited to their own purposes and by the use of materials taken from untypical years. Generalizations as to the rise and fall in a trend, or as to the national significance of a local indicator, he should perceive, must be related precisely to their context in time and place. Having made his corrections, he should seek his solution in taking as much from either side as he is able.

The problems outlined in this sample controversy are in many ways typical of those which arise in connection with the major issues in eighteenth- and nineteenth-century economic history. The student will encounter 'optimists' and 'pessimists' not only in argument over working-class living standards but also locked in debate over the severity of the 'Great Depression' of 1873–96, the rationality or otherwise of British foreign investment in the late nineteenth century, or the degree of stagnation experienced by the British economy between 1919 and 1939. The difficulties over the areas of agreement, the statistics, the time-frame, and the selection of material will be encountered with these and many other disputed issues. The student who learns to recognize these snares as they approach and to apply the countermeasures will have made a useful beginning in the quest for the first class answer in economic history.

Naturally, the recommendations put forward in this essay can constitute no magic formula for success. For one thing, there will be immense variations in the way students employ the stratagems outlined here. For another, these stratagems, on a certain reading, represent merely *some* preferences of *one* teacher of economic history. Yet, in a subject feared by many for its apparent complexity, there is room for a measure of reassurance. This is not to imply that the advice given does not possess its own elements of controversy; it most certainly does, notably that section dealing with the treatment of statistical materials by the student. However, within a university system which has not yet achieved a wide spread of multi-disciplinary education, it would seem merely realistic to accept the pupil's necessary limitations while still indicating methods by which he might deal with the subject's knottier aspects. The pupil is, after all, an amateur and should not be judged, nor judge himself, by the standards of the professional. This raises a further point: if there is a place for a certain humility on the part of the student when confronted with the intricacies of the subject, this should not be carried too far. The humility which is really an unthinking dismissal of all things economic as impenetrably involved, the humility which breeds a paralysed suspension of judgement, is entirely inappropriate and wholly unnecessary. If economic history is intricate, it is not notably more so than any other branch of historical inquiry in which research is active. Similarly, it unlocks a good many of its secrets to the student who approaches its problems with an unflustered common sense and a certain capacity for sustained logical thought.

Notes

1. As general reading for this period, see particularly: T. S. Ashton, *The Industrial Revolution* (1948); P. Deane and W. A. Cole, *British Economic Growth 1688–1959* (1962); P. Deane, *The First Industrial Revolution* (1965); M. Flinn, *The Origins of the Industrial Revolution* (1966); R. M. Hartwell (ed.), *The Causes of the Industrial Revolution in England* (1967); P. Mathias, *The First Industrial Nation* (1969).

2. See particularly: J. D. Chambers, *The Workshop of the World 1820–80* (1961); S. G. Checkland, *The Rise of Industrial Society in England 1815–85* (1964); P. Deane and W. A. Cole, *British Economic Growth 1688–1959*; E. J. Hobsbawm, *Industry and Empire* (1968).
3. Useful accounts of this period are provided by: W. Ashworth, *An Economic History of England 1870–1939* (1960); A. L. Levine, *Industrial Retardation in Britain 1880 1914* (1967); R. S. Sayers, *A History of Economic Change in England 1880–1939* (1967).
4. See: D. H. Aldcroft and H. W. Richardson, *The British Economy 1870–1939* (1969) for a selection of the most recent writings offering a revisionist view of the 'Inter-war Depression'; Also C. L. Mowat, *Britain between the Wars* (1956); W. A. Lewis, *Economic Survey 1919–39* (1949); A. J. Youngson, *The British Economy 1920–57* (1960).
5. Peter Mathias, in *New Movements in the Study and Teaching of History*, ed. Martin Ballard, (1970), p. 80.
6. See: D. McCloskey, 'Did Victorian Britain Fail', *Economic History Review*, 23 (1970), pp. 446–59.
7. M. Edelstein, in ed. D. McCloskey, *Essays on a Mature Economy: Britain after 1840*, (1971), pp. 83–111.
8. D. McCloskey (ed.), *Essays on a Mature Economy: Britain after 1840* (1971) pp. 285–304.
9. Mathias, in *New Movements in the Study and Teaching of History*, p. 90.
10. There is, of course, an overlap here since the 'new economic historians' are doing nothing if not building 'models' by mathematical means.
11. See W. W. Rostow, *The Stages of Economic Growth* (1960).
12. *ibid*, p. 4.
13. J. Z. Young, *Doubt & Certainty in Science. A Biologist's Reflections on the Brain* (1951), p. 86 cited by A. Gerschenkron, *Continuity in History*, (1968).
14. A. Gerschenkron, *Continuity in History* (1968), p. 46.
15. See above pp. 48, 61, for instance.
16. J. D. Chambers and G. E. Mingay, *The Agricultural Revolution* (1966).
17. D. C. Coleman, 'Industrial Growth and Industrial Revolutions' *Economica* 23 (1956), pp 1–20; P. Deane and H. J. Habakkuk, in *The Economics of Take-off into Sustained Growth*, ed. W. W. Rostow, (1963), pp. 63–82; S. Kuznets, in *The Economics of Take-off into Sustained Growth*, pp. 22–43, and, for com-

parative assessments for several countries, S. Kuznets, 'Quantitative Aspects of the Economic Growth of Nations', V and VI, *Economic Development and Cultural Change* (July 1960 and July, 1961).

18. H. J. Habakkuk, 'English Population during the Eighteenth Century', *Economic History Review*, 6 (1953) pp. 117–133 and T. McKeown and R. G. Brown, 'The Medical Evidence related to English Population Changes in the Eighteenth Century', *Population Studies*, (1955).
19. A. E. Musson, 'British Industrial Growth during the Great Depression', *Economic History Review*, 15 (1963 and 1964) pp. 529–533 and D. J. Coppock', 'British Industrial Growth during the Great Depression: A Pessimist's View', *Economic History Review*, 17 (1964) pp. 389–403.
20. E. J. Hobsbawm, 'The British Standard of Living 1790–1850', *Economic History Review*, 10 (1957) pp 46–61 and R. M. Hartwell, 'The Rising Standard of Living in England, 1800–50', *Economic History Review*, 13 (1961) pp. 397–416. In addition, see F. Engels, *The Condition of the Working Class in England* (ed. W. O. Henderson and W. H. Chaloner, 1958); E. Royston Pike, *Human Documents of the Industrial Revolution* (1966); N. Smelser, *Social Change in the Industrial Revolution* (1959); E. P. Thompson, *The Making of the English Working Class* (1963).
21. E. J. Hobsbawm, *Industry and Empire* (1968), p. 74. My italics.
22. J. E. Williams, 'The British Standard of Living 1750–1850', *Economic History Review*, 19 (1966), p. 586.
23. E. J. Hobsbawm, 'The British Standard of Living 1790–1850', *Economic History Review*, 10 (1957), p. 56.
24. R. S. Neale, 'The Standard of Living 1780–1844: A Regional and Class Study', *Economic History Review*, 19 (1966), pp. 590–605 and T. R. Gourvish, 'The Cost of Living in Glasgow in the Early Nineteenth Century', *Economic History Review*, 25 (1972), pp. 65–80.
25. H. Perkin, *The Origins of Modern British Society* (1969), p. 137.
26. See particularly: A. Briggs, *Victorian Cities* (1963).
27. G. Rudé, *The Crowd in History* (1964), p. 79.

6 *History of the United States*

Hugh Brogan

Necessary evils, examinations in American history are like other members of the species, except in one important respect. The techniques that help candidates to do themselves justice in, say, English medieval history, also apply to the history of the United States; and both subjects require a stretching of the imagination. But of course the imaginative exercise is somewhat different for the two subjects. The prime purpose of this chapter must therefore be to suggest the most useful approach to the uniqueness of American history. Yet a few preliminary remarks on the more mundane side of the problem remain in order. If they seem familiar, so much the better: they will illustrate the fundamental unity of historical study.

Essentially, the most dependable techniques for producing a good candidate in an examination are those which produce a man or woman, boy or girl, well-grounded in a particular subject. Examinations and education are not so far separated as some people think, even though examinations can only test certain types of achievement. Of course there can be no doubt as to their comparative importance. Education is the thing. It trains people for examinations only incidentally. Still, it does train them, and a well-educated person should be a well-prepared examinee. Some skill in the lesser art indicates some skill in the greater, and by starting with examination techniques here we can hope not only to put a distasteful topic behind us quickly, but at the same time to find a way into the greater and much more difficult topic of education.

I suppose the first rule for a good candidate ought to be calmness of mind. Nothing – not even affectionate anxiety – can justify the parent, teacher or friend who increases a candidate's emotional tension before an important exam. 'Young ladies,' observed Jane Austen's Mr Woodhouse, 'are delicate plants.' So are young gentlemen, when it comes to examinations. If we are honest with ourselves and others we must all admit that we know how easy it is, in our youth, to be anxious and depressed at the thought of failure, whether in love, life or learning. We want to leave the nest, and yet the process of facing the world for the first time has its terrors. Fortunately the joy of life seen reassures most of us, and we find that we are at least as capable as anyone else of getting a job, a family and a home, and a measure of satisfaction from these good things. However, at the age when examinations loom large this triumphant discovery lies mostly in the future. The examination is seen as a searching scrutiny of our spiritual and intellectual fitness for life. If it were such a scrutiny, of course it would be reasonable, indeed inevitable, to dread it: 'Use every man after his desert,' said Hamlet, that experienced undergraduate, 'and who shall 'scape whipping?' Happily, an examination is only a very elementary test of knowledge and abilities. The belief that it is anything more is a mere frightening illusion, bred by the natural modesty, or the timidity, of inexperienced young people. We create our own hobgoblins, summon our own nightmares. It is the duty of our associates to do nothing to encourage us in these alarming practices. A good breakfast is one sound preparation for an examination; another is a day of rest before the ordeal; and another, I am inclined to think, at least where history is concerned, is to forget a bit. Too much information is sometimes more of a handicap than too little. At least an evenly spread measure of ignorance won't stop you seeing the wood for the trees, unless it is also spread very thick. (It is also a good idea to avoid metaphors – they tend to get mixed, like these two.) More important, the candidate who comes into the examination-room crammed with information on a few preferred topics (since he can't be crammed on everything) may make several ghastly errors in his determination to show it. In a mad anxiety to put down all he knows about, say, the American Civil War in forty minutes – an impossible aspiration – he (or she – girls are at least as prone to this fault as boys) may not notice that the question requires a rather different answer, as did one I set recently: 'Could slavery have been ended peacefully?' To answer this satisfactorily one has to realize that it is above all a question about slavery, and, rephrased, amounts to this: 'We all know that in fact it took a civil war to end slavery, and that slavery was one of the chief causes of that war. But supposing – as was at least possible – that the war could have been postponed, or averted altogether, did slavery have any prospect of evolving into something else, namely, real freedom for the slaves?' This is a quite difficult enough question to answer in forty minutes, since it involves an analysis of a complex social institution, without dragging in an irrelevant analysis of the various factors that together brought war in 1861.[1]

Or a candidate may be completely thrown by the failure of a pet topic to turn up in the paper at all. I once had to comfort a very beautiful girl, reduced to tears because there was no question on Chateaubriand in a paper on early nineteenth-century French history. It is much better to be able to approach all, or almost all, the questions with an equal degree of expertise: the intelligence gets freer play, since one can choose the questions that suit one best out of a wide range; and of course someone with a proper knowledge of American history from the seventeenth or eighteenth century to the present day is in just this position of versatility. Since it is quite impossible for a candidate to know in equal depth all the answers to a paper consisting of twenty or more questions, he ought perhaps to aim at an equal shallowness. At the very least (since this counsel comes a little too near to being a plug for laziness, glibness and superficiality) he ought to have forgotten a little, especially about his pet subjects. He may write better, and choose his questions with more discretion, if his mind is not too filled up with them.

Nothing wearies an examiner more than two closely related errors: the failure to read a question carefully enough, and the determination to serve up a prepared answer. There really is no substitute, if you want to achieve your best performance, for care in reading and thinking about the question-paper. It's not a matter of searching out subtle traps. Most good examination questions are easy, or at any rate easier than they look at first glance, if you let yourself understand them. There is a great tendency among students, whether at school or university, automatically to reply 'I don't know' to any question. It saves them the trouble of listening. This shocking habit is absolutely fatal in an examination. For example, some years ago I set the question, ' "The cause of the American Revolution cannot be determined by one who confines his investigation to the American field alone" (Charles M. Andrews). Illustrate.' This question was simplicity itself. A calm, competent, moderately well-informed candidate would need only to list and discuss a few incidents, selected from an embarrassment of riches, that occurred between 1763 and 1776. For example, it is universal knowledge that one of the causes of the American Revolution was the taxation policy of the British government. The cry 'no taxation without representation', is a cliché that the most slothful student must have come across. It is also pretty widely known that no British ministry, with the very partial exception of Rockingham's, which repealed the Stamp Act, had the statesmanship to deal with the crisis.[2] They all tried very hard, but their failure is a matter of record. It is easy enough to state this, and even easier to illustrate it, with reference, say, to the collapse of Lord Chatham or the circumstances which led to an alliance between the intelligent but weak Lord North and the virtuously obstinate George III. A little reading in any of the short, excellent paperbacks available[3] – or a good knowledge of the Declaration of Independence – would furnish plenty more, rather more complex, but still easily grasped illustrative material. In short, it is impossible to imagine that a candidate who had done a little – only a little – real work on the Amercan Revolution could find this question difficult. But most of the candidates I had to mark had come into the room with the old fiendish determination to tackle all the largest and most difficult questions – in this case, the question of all the causes, and the complete nature, of the American Revolution. The fact that they had been asked something much easier escaped their notice.[4] They wasted their time and mine, and were marked down accordingly. Please, please, *please* read the question, and then answer *it*, and not some other.

If you are calm enough to read the paper and understand it, you ought also to be calm enough to choose the easy questions. Every examiner has in his time succumbed to the temptation of putting in one or two difficult but interesting problems in the hope that the cleverer candidate will tackle them: perhaps unconsciously we hope that young, fresh brains can teach us something about problems that baffle our veteran but weary intelligence.[5] Unhappily the clever candidates are clever enough to know a quagmire when they see one; it is the incompetent who plunge in. There is, it is true, a difficulty here: ignorance may mistake itself, and think it knows the answer when it doesn't. But the earnest candidate, who has worked fairly hard, will certainly find, in any decent paper, enough questions to which he *knows* he knows the answer. Those are the ones to attempt. If you are unlucky, and a difficult question must be tackled, leave it to the last. It is the questions you find easy which are going to help you – don't risk having to skimp them from fatigue . . . and in any case, *leave enough time.*

Mind you, the sense in which any of us 'knows' the answer to historical questions is a somewhat special one. The best candidate, like the best historian, is the one who knows so much that he knows how scanty is his knowledge, like Isaac Newton, who saw himself as a child trifling on the shore of the ocean of truth. Such an attitude leads to tentative statements, qualified and wary, supported not by ringing assertion and wild generalizations but by carefully chosen and modestly advanced factual arguments. Of course it is possible, indeed highly desirable, to put forward even cautious arguments with flair and intuition; but essentially the art of examination answers, like the art of history itself, consists in advancing tenable and testable hypotheses.[6] Literary criticism, F. R. Leavis has taught us, asks, 'This is so, isn't it?' and gets the answer, 'Yes, but. . . .' A similar delicacy marks all the best historical thinking, even if it is well camouflaged under the bounce of a Macaulay or the suave omniscience of a Gibbon. It is an agreeable quality, and has the advantage of being within the reach of us all, at least in our better moments. And are we not all modest on examination day?

The easy questions once selected, it remains only to tackle them – as many as the rubric requires, no more, no less. Absurd that it should be necessary to say this, but many are the clever fools who, apparently, imagine they can defy the rubric and get away with it. Again I say, be modest: no candidate is likely to be so original and profound that one essay by him on one topic will be worth three or four (or whatever the examiners require) by another candidate on three or four topics. Partly it's a matter of common justice: if one candidate takes three hours over two questions while his fellows, as asked, take three over three, and the examiners don't penalize the odd man out, he has given himself an unfair advantage. (In such an examination it would be equally unwise to answer four questions in three hours.) No, you must accept the fact that the examiners will decide to test your intelligence and your beginner's knowledge in a particular way, and that way must be followed docilely. It is, no doubt, in many respects an inadequate test. Still, that inadequacy is equal for all. Every candidate ought to be mature and efficient enough to give the right amount of time to each question. It's a matter of the methodical intellect, a valuable quality which exams are quite right to test and thus to encourage. It's a matter of training oneself to know what one wants to say and then saying it. Best to say it elegantly, of course; but any candidate who sticks firmly to the matter in hand, and has perhaps practised a little, will find it easy enough to satisfy himself and his examiners.

Yet sticking to the matter in hand – relevance – is another of those concepts to which candidates too often pay mere lip-service. Scholars who devote their lives to trying to see problems clearly in all their bearings cannot endure waffle – that is, anything which impedes a clear view of the truth unnecessarily. So much is going to come between us and the truth anyway. It is of no use dragging in impressive allusions to topics which have little or nothing to do with the case. (I should perhaps admit that this is a vice of which even now I try in vain to break myself entirely.) The examination is too short – the examiner will necessarily conclude that you are trying to cover up your ignorance by your elegance. You must send your thought naked into the arena. If you have got it right then you want to make the fact as plain as possible. If you've got it wrong you shouldn't be doing the question. Be calm, be sensible, be modest – even if you are a genius. It need only be this once. The point is to pass the examination with credit, not to prove that you are the new Thucydides. It is like a driving test – you want to pass, not to gratify your ego by brilliant daring.

Finally, don't presume on your examiners' powers of extra-sensory perception. All too many pupils of mine, in essays, and, I fear, in examinations, have shown a fatal tendency to say one thing while meaning another. Apparently they have expected to be read between the lines – which is arrogant and therefore silly. If you write, 'The Declaration of Independence was signed on 3 July 1766' it is no good expecting the examiner to be sure you *meant* to write '4 July 1776'. He, not being a mind-reader, can only mark you down for making a mistake (especially as the Declaration was not in fact signed until 2 August 1776).[7] Nor can an examiner be depended on to sense the real extent of your knowledge through a cloudy prose style or an unreadable hand.

Bear these negative precepts in mind, and examination papers become mere routine. For example, suppose the question to tackle is 'To what extent was the American Revolution revolutionary?' Here is a perfect specimen of a question that is deadly to candidates without a firm grasp of essentials, but easy to those who do not lose their heads. They will, as good historians, try to go to the heart of the matter. It would be easy to get bogged down in a discussion of what exactly is meant by 'revolution' and 'revolutionary' nowadays, or what was meant by them in the eighteenth century. An American author, Crane Brinton, in his *Anatomy of Revolution,* got hopelessly stuck. Such traps must be avoided, and the intelligent candidate will have his own methods of escape. Two points occur to me at once. One may remark, with absolute sense, that the American Revolution did not acquire its name for nothing. It conformed, fairly precisely, to what the eighteenth century, brought up on the legend of 1688, expected of a revolution. Secondly, any convulsion which altered social, constitutional and legal forms, touched off civil and international wars, and left an indelible mark on the beliefs and consciousness of a people (not to mention the ruin and exile of the American Tories, which led to the foundation of English-speaking Canada) may conveniently be described as revolutionary: it is not necessary to inquire whether it conformed to a Marxist or Brintonian model. Illustrations of the revolutionary changes should certainly be attempted, from knowledge which any adequately prepared examinee will have at his finger-tips. One might glance at the manner in which the preamble to the Declaration of Independence carried the tradition of English liberalism forward to new and, for the time, startling formulations, not at all acceptable even to such a rising radical as the young Jeremy Bentham (whose own brand of liberalism, be it admitted, was even more novel than Jefferson's).

But no answer would be complete which did not also find time to consider the point of view of the devil's advocate. Here the most important argument, if not indeed the only one, is that the continuity of American life and thought before, during and after the revolution was so marked and so important that it quite dwarfs the elements of novelty and discontinuity which we call revolutionary. The constitution which crowned the revolution, says the advocate, was in a sense merely the rationalization and consummation of the developments of more than a century and a half. Again the illustrations to be brought in support of this argument will occur to all conscientious students. Their only cares will be to avoid weighing down their answers with too much detail, and to keep within their time limit. Otherwise the thing practically writes itself, until the conclusion: which you will have to work out for yourselves.[8]

So much for negative advice, all of it applicable to other subjects as well as to American history. Read the questions – choose the easy ones – stick to the point – obey the rubric – and, if you have worked seriously, and have not allowed yourself to succumb to panic over little things, you will not fall below a sound performance. We, however, are concerned with more than that, with the problem of attaining one's best.

History, like most true art and all true study, is, as I have already said, a quest for the heart of the matter. All such quests are at times dusty affairs. We need either a keen delight in the chase or a clear perception of its value to us (preferably both) to persist to the end. This consideration applies as much to the study of American history as to anything else.

First, then, if you want to do creditably in an examination on American history, you must satisfy yourself that you know why you have taken up the subject, and that your commitment to it is strong enough to keep you going until the day of the ordeal. This requires a long view, self-knowledge, and a clear understanding of what you are letting yourself in for. Only the last point can usefully be discussed here: for it is up to you yourself to decide which subject will bring out the best in you, which will most contribute to your education. Presume I am an honest shopkeeper: what follows is my sales talk. Only you yourself can decide whether you want to buy.

In the first place, it must be acknowledged that American history demands an exercise of the imagination which presents peculiar difficulties to English people. They arise from the links and gulfs between our two societies. For example, numberless jokes have been made about the barrier raised by our common language – jokes deriving from the fact that it both helps and hinders understanding. Words are, no doubt, the best introduction to men and nations, but they are only the beginning. There comes a point when an easy understanding can be a potent source of an easy misunderstanding. To share a language is a great thing; it must not lead us to forget that there are many things we do not share.

So anyone seriously interested in America might well begin by grappling with the language. English today is soaked in what were once Americanisms, but it remains a distinct dialect, and American is as individual as ever. Speakers of the two tongues have no difficulty in understanding each other at a superficial level (though they usually find it impossible to speak each other's lingo accurately); but to go beyond that demands work – work easier and pleasanter than learning French, Latin or German, but work all the same: work that will pay off in examinations.

The most agreeable guide to American is undoubtedly H. L. Mencken. His *The American Language* is an extraordinarily rich compendium. It contains a valuable comparative section on English and American; but, even more useful, his book as a whole conveys an extraordinarily precise sense of the quiddity of American – of its individuality, not merely by comparison with the mother tongue, but in itself. Through this quiddity we can begin to catch the quiddity of the American people too. Take, for example, this list, compiled from Mencken:

ash-can
billboard
drygoods-store
cornstarch
elevator
frame-house
garbage-incinerator
huckster

instalment-plan	pitcher
jack-rabbit	roomer
katy-did	suspenders
long-distance	tenderloin
molasses	undershirt
necktie	vaudeville
outhouse	whiskey-sour

None of these terms is slang or jargon or obscure; all are American. Taken together as a theme for meditation they begin to suggest a certain flavour in American life – say, the flavour of the Middle West, well worth catching, and easily caught: but it will elude the careless. The rest may find that explorations like this slowly breed that love of a subject, that fascination, without which no really first class performance is possible, except as a quite unpredictable fluke. Soldiers, sailors and examinees must know what they fight for and love what they know: it is my business to suggest ways of coming to love America and American history.[9]

Sea, air and money cut the English off from the Americans, and yet films, television, books, newspapers and tourism link us to them. Of course not all that passes for Americanization nowadays is, in fact, simply American: much of it is mere modernization, the universally necessary results of a particular technological culture; one of the American historian's problems is distinguishing between the two. Still there is no denying that the impact of the United States on the modern world, and perhaps especially on Great Britain, has been enormous, while it is still very difficult to visit America regularly enough to get a reliable knowledge of it (though fortunately it grows easier all the time). This combination of knowledge and ignorance, availability and inaccessibility, is a peculiarly teasing phenomenon to which the student must be constantly alert. Otherwise he may be fatally trapped into believing that he knows what he does not, or into supposing that casual prejudice, opinion and misinformation is understanding and knowledge.[10]

These hurdles passed, the real differences between England and America come into view, and must at times prove daunting. There are so many of them, and the ripest scholar will never be able to discount them, or cease to discover new ones. To list a few: America is so large, both in terms of geographical extent and population. Her people are both immensely various in origins and surprisingly uniform in culture (except that they are also surprisingly diversified). Her federal, political and legal system is utterly unlike anything in England; it both conceals the great degree of centralization achieved in this century and ensures that, for good and ill, centralization will never go to English lengths. The climate, arctic in winter and sub-tropical in summer over most of the continent, may not have the direct influence on institutions that Montesquieu might have predicted, but has certainly conditioned the manners and customs of the citizens profoundly.[11] Above all, I think, the ancient democratic culture of America, innovative, anti-élitist, individualist, both explains and embodies the radical difference between the English and the American soul – or, if you like, social psychology. The English have what may be called an historical culture: not specifically aristocratic, monarchical, imperialist or democratic – not even purely nationalistic – but a culture shaped by a thousand years of life on an unconquered island. Norman wars, Anglo-Welsh, Anglo-Scottish, Anglo-Irish, Anglo-Spanish, Anglo-French, Anglo-German wars, civil wars – none of these (still less the union of the three parts of Great Britain since 1707) have seriously impaired the continuity of English life, or counterbalanced its role in shaping the English consciousness. America shares some of these roots, some of these continuities; but on the whole a nation founded in such decisive experiences as the Atlantic migration, the American Revolution, the American Civil War – a revolution in itself – has differentiated itself quite decisively from its parent. Like many parents, Great Britain cannot always recognize the fact. For example, there is a bad habit, which is manifested every presidential year, of British commentators expressing grave anxieties about the choice the American people are about to make. This time, it is solemnly hinted, they are about to go wrong. It is pure cheek. The Americans have been electing their leaders, one way or another, since the seventeenth century, and with the full apparatus of representative democracy since the early nineteenth century. They are veteran democrats. The English, who only achieved universal male suffrage just before the First World War, have nothing to teach the American people in this field and a great deal to learn.[12]

If these are some of the problems of studying American history, they are clearly also some of the rewards. History is a form of travel: it broadens the mind. Whether one takes up the study of the American past because of interest in the American present, or because of the subject's own fascination, or for all three reasons together, one has already demonstrated the historian's most important trait: the will to look beyond the confines of one's own time and place. The special pleasures of American history do not lie in the succession of heroes and battles, even though the natives themselves gloat over every skirmish in their short past, and sometimes seem to think their every politician was a statesman. A European will merely note that, even so, the supply is rather small compared to that of his own continent. No, the essence of American history is the discovery of a people, and the exploration of the intricacies of its life and organization as they display themselves down the years. The more you study the American Revolution, for example, the more you will be struck by the extent to which the political incidents of that saga were determined by the passions, habits and expectations of the people. English policy threw itself across the line of natural American development, and was minced very fine as a result. The student, then, finds himself necessarily drawn to a sociological approach to history, since the spectacle he confronts is always one of a society determining itself; and this, though perhaps dry and demanding at first taste, proves in the end the most imaginatively satisfying of all approaches, since all is grist to its mill, whether popular songs or the popular diet, wage-rates or tax-rates, heroic speeches or heroic actions.

No one will study American history with profit for very long who cannot respond to books with titles such as *The Political Economy of Slavery*, *The Ideological Origins of the American Revolution*, *The Life of the Mind in America*, *The Transportation Revolution*, or *The Rise of the City*.[13] In these and similar works is to be found the essence of American history. Perhaps to many students the discovery is not worth making. But to some, to me, for instance, who as a child first met history in the story of how dark Xerxes came to gaze on the destruction of his armada beside Salamis, the endless pursuit of the truth about the American people is as rewarding a study as history has to offer. To those who share, in greater or less degree, this pleasure, mere examinations in the subject need have no terrors.

Notes

1. Good books on the topic of American slavery are so numerous that it is difficult to choose among them. But the following should give a good idea of the nature of chattel slavery, and enable a reader to see for himself what the difficulties are in speculating about its possible, no-Civil-War future: David Brion Davis, *The Problems of Slavery in Western Culture,* (Ithaca, New York 1966) (Pelican 1970); Winthrop D. Jordan, *White over Black* (Chapel Hill 1968); Kenneth M. Stampp, *The Peculiar Institution* (New York 1956); Eugene D. Genovese, *The Political Economy of Slavery* (New York 1965); Stanley M. Elkins, *Slavery* (Chicago 1959) (paperback, New York 1963).
2. The best examination of British statemanship, or lack of it, is still Charles R. Ritcheson, *British Politics and the American Revolution* (University of Oklahoma Press 1954). Ritcheson detects a steadily-growing conservatism in British reactions to crises in the increasingly radicalized colonies.
3. Charles M. Andrews, *The Colonial Background of the American Revolution* (Yale paperbound, New Haven and London 1967); I. R. Christie, *Crisis of Empire* (1966); Bernhard Knollenberg, *Origin of the American Revolution* (1961).
4. No doubt some of them insisted on parading their large, vacuous answers to (unasked) large, vacuous questions because, whether from idleness or distaste for the minutiae of history, they had reduced history to a handful of convenient formulations, like the notorious rise of the middle class, which can explain any event in any epoch. But the idle are just the idle, while people with no taste for minutiae ought not to be doing history. I am concerned with more promising candidates than these.
5. For example, I once set, 'How important was the first Wilson administration in the history of the American party system?'

This is a difficult and complex question on which I have strong views, but the research on the matter is still remote from the knowledge of undergraduates, and is indeed very incomplete, so it was not surprising that few attempted this question and that still fewer did it well.

6. An important book which displays all these qualities is Stanley Elkins's *Slavery* (see note 2, above). Mr Elkins, with great verve and lucidity, advances several important new ideas about the nature of American chattel slavery. His theories are based on sound scholarship as well as great intelligence; but throughout his book the author, implicitly and explicitly, invites argument – which he got in plenty (see Ann J. Lane, ed., *The Debate Over Slavery* [University of Illinois 1971]).
7. The legend of the Fourth of July is discussed most entertainingly in Daniel Boorstin, *The National Experience* (1966), pp. 377–80.
8. The most stimulating discussion of the American Revolution in its context is R. R. Palmer, *The Age of the Democratic Revolution* (Princeton 1959 and 1964), I and II. He sees it as truly revolutionary, being a part of the general transformation of the Atlantic world at the end of the eighteenth century.
9. The two cannot really be separated. This holds true for all societies, of course: past and present are inextricable; but the time-span of American history is so comparatively short, and the constants in it are so numerous, that it is especially important to realize this interdependence. Never trust a guide to the American past who is not equally concerned with the United States today.
10. Much the best way of dealing with this problem is to go to America yourself, for as long a visit as possible. Failing that, or in supplementation to it, you could do worse than read some of the many books specially directed to explaining America to England. Of these the best are written by Sir Denis Brogan. See, especially, *The American Political System* (1933); *U.S.A.* (1941); *The American Problem* (1944).
11. I forbear to put in the body of my text the remark that nowadays the citizens are air-conditioned.
12. The great issues touched on in this paragraph are still best studied, at least to begin with, in such classic works as Alexis de Tocqueville, *Democracy in America*; James Bryce, *The American Commonwealth*; Frederick Jackson Turner, *The Significance of the Frontier in American History*.
13. By Eugene Genovese (New York 1965); Bernard Bailyn

(Cambridge, Mass. 1967); Perry Miller (1966); George R. Taylor (New York 1951) and Arthur Schlesinger (New York 1933) respectively.

Further Reading

Many of the chief works of American historiography are, sad to say, very badly written. This is not true of the books in the following highly selective list. It omits many topics and authors, but the titles it does include are both important and beguiling – just what history ought to be. New readers begin here.

The American Heritage Book of Indians (New York 1961).
William Bradford, *Of Plymouth Plantation*, 1620–1647, ed. S. E. Morison (New York 1966).
Arthur M. Schlesinger, *The Birth of the Nation: a Portrait of the American People on the Eve of Independence* (New York 1968).
Alexander Hamilton, James Madison and John Jay, *The Federalist*, ed. Jacob E. Cook (Middletown, Conn. 1961).
Herbert Agar, *The United States: the Presidents, the Parties and the Constitution* (London, 1950).
Richard Hofstadter, *The American Political Tradition* (New York 1948).
Arthur M. Schlesinger, Jr., *The Age of Jackson* (Boston, Mass. 1945).
Francis Trollope, *Domestic Manners of the Americans*, ed. Donald Smalley (New York 1949).
Bernard De Voto, *The Year of Decision* (Boston 1961).
Stephen Vincent Benet, *John Brown's Body* (New York 1928).
Margaret Leech, *Reveille in Washington, 1860–65* (London, 1942).
W. J. Cash, *The Mind of the South* (New York 1941).
Henry Adams, *The Education of Henry Adams* (Boston 1961).
Mark Sullivan, *Our Times: the United States 1900–1925* (New York and London 1926–1935).
Andrew Sinclair, *Prohibition* (London, 1962).
D. W. Brogan, *The Era of Franklin D. Roosevelt* (New York 1950).
T. Harry Williams, *Huey Long* (London, 1970).

7 *The Expansion of Europe, Imperial, African and Asian History since c.1800*

Ronald Hyam

I

For about five centuries the Chinese Government prescribed an 'eight-legged essay' as a prominent feature of their examination for entry to the civil service. This was an essay of eight paragraphs and a specified number of calligraphic characters. The exercise required proficiency in discussing a Confucian philosophical theme within this formal structural framework. Its eight paragraphs conformed to the following pattern: analysis of the theme, amplification of the theme, explanation, post-explanation, argument (i), reassertion of theme, argument (ii) and argument (iii). Eventually this form of writing put such a premium on stereotyped techniques of antithetical structure at the expense of knowledge and content that it became a notorious symbol of all that was rigid and stylized in old imperial China, and its abolition was decreed in 1901. The opprobrium with which it was denounced was not entirely fair. It was said, with little real justification, that those trained to do well in such stylistic exercises became incapable either of determined management of affairs or of conceiving change and reform in government. The eight-legged essay became a scapegoat to explain the slowness of China's nineteenth-century modernization.[1] This was rather silly, if only because Mao Tse-tung was perfectly capable of writing a proficient eight-legged essay as well as leading one of the most remarkable revolutionary movements of all time. Besides, there were many other and more deep-seated obstacles to change in Manchu China.

Now whilst it would be absurd to suggest that a model

historical essay could be based upon a blueprint derived from the eight-legged essay in classical Chinese, I begin by referring to it since it focuses attention on an important fundamental of history essay writing, namely its formal structure. Provided that we bear in mind content as well as form, it is a useful starting-point for discussion.

II

When I was an undergraduate, I did actually ask my director of studies the question 'What makes a first-class essay?' He replied, 'The ability to see the answer to a given problem as a rounded whole.' What he was chiefly concerned to do, I think, was to direct my attention (at least as an ideal for which to work) to the supreme importance of a sustained theme or line of argument, of a perspective wide in space and deep in time, of a comprehensive grasp of the issues involved, and of the necessity of differentiating between the quintessential and the merely important, sorting out the fundamental and subsidiary points of explanation, allocating them their appropriate significance, and finally relating them together in such a way as to make a pattern at once clear, controlled, balanced and complete. One could not hope quickly to succeed in these objectives, but they excitingly signposted the route to improvement.

The good historian is, like a good architect or composer, making meaningful patterns. Each works to some extent within set limits. The architect of a cathedral cannot ignore its liturgical function. The composer who sets the liturgy to music cannot alter the words. The historian cannot alter the ascertainable facts. Yet within the same limits and working with similar materials, not all cathedrals, nor all settings of the *Gloria,* nor even all historical analyses are equally good. The difference is usually structural. Structure is of the very essence of all creative work. There is nothing so satisfying as a structure (architectural, musical, literary or what you will) which has enough detailed complexity to challenge one's intellectual interest, but such a grand total clarity as to be overwhelmingly exciting in its convincing simplicity. Even though it may perforce be the product of only a week's work, an historical essay must have a structure too. It will not be a polished production

– further thought and new knowledge will probably modify it substantially – but it is none the less a serious attempt at organizing material and arranging ideas. Thus it cannot in any case be totally shapeless; but the better its organization and arrangement, the firmer its structure and the more convincing its pattern, the more effective it will be as an essay.

In writing history, the framework can be chosen. The patterns do not pre-exist. The material used in research by an historian of the British Empire, for example, will for the most part be organized in no more coherent or rational way than that imposed by the filing systems of government departments. From these the historian abstracts certain information, and, in writing it up, re-organizes it into a completely different framework. The sixth-former or undergraduate does much the same thing: quarrying material from the books on his reading list, treating them as grist to his mill, refusing to be mesmerized by them. If he wishes to write something authentic (in the literal sense of self-made) and if he aspires to be anything more than high quality blotting-paper, soaking up his teacher's views, he ought, at least over some stretches of time, to read very hard indeed, and always in a ruthlessly critical spirit. The undergraduate has the opportunity to read on a scale which is never possible before entering a university and which is unlikely ever to be possible again, even if he becomes a professional academic. But, of course, he must not simply read, mark and learn. He must also, and above all else, *inwardly digest*. This needs time and thought; if achieved, the learning can be left largely to take care of itself. If, through wide reading complemented by thinking, a problem can be seen as 'a rounded whole', the historian acquires a built-in check against taking up untenable stances, and places a revealing distance between himself and the materials he uses. As A. J. P. Taylor once said, the good historian should ride the waves and not swim in them.

The apprentice historian, then, will want to address himself to the problems of organizing material, and to experiment with alternative structural types of essay. There are, for example, obvious differences between the way one treats a nearly-monocausal and a multiple-cause explanation, and there are differences in technique between both and a comparison of historical developments in two states or a review of another historian's explanation. For convenience, these sample structures might be labelled respectively citadel, caravan, comparison and critique.[2] If the problem under discussion is one of the rare kind which lends itself nearly to a single-cause answer, the appropriate structure is a 'citadel' type: one main point massively buttressed into a central position by all the supporting evidence (statistics, succinct contemporary quotations, and so forth), with the subsidiary defences laid out more superficially in its shadow. The 'caravan' type (in the American sense of a waggon-train) will be a structure with a succession of more evenly weighted components. A 'comparative' structure integrates the different characteristic aspects of the countries or people compared at each step, and is not simply an essay broken into two largely unrelated halves. A 'critique' is a dangerous type: it tends to deal in historiography rather than history; its chief fault is that it often leaves big gaps – either not making plain exactly what the author has said, or sidestepping a crucial part of his argument, sometimes because the critic is blind and sometimes because the argument does not perfectly fit the attack he planned to launch.

If a problem is capable of a simple explanation, this fact should not be obscured by padding it out. It is as bad to turn simple problems into complex ones as it is to over-simplify complexities. Questions such as 'Why did the Imperial Federation movement fail to provide closer economic and political links between the British colonies in the late nineteenth century?' could in fact (like questions about the failure of the South African National Congress or the League of Nations) be largely answered with a reasoned case stating that it never stood a chance of succeeding. The failure of many projects is implicit in the fact that they were inherently unsound and impracticable; it is not true that they were splendid ideas which were ruined only by human folly, stupid management, bad luck, lack of commitment by leaders, unforeseen vicious opposition by vested interests or poor publicity. In cases like this, the real question is not 'Why did they fail?', but 'Why did able men ever expect them to succeed?'[3] If you can boldly answer the original question in some such fundamental way, do so. You may then reveal a more interesting general question about human behaviour. In any case, there are quite enough really complex problems left to argue about.

One such question is the Partition of Africa. Let us suppose that you are about to write an essay on the British part in the Partition. Which of the four types – comparison, critique, citadel or caravan (or any other which occurs to you) – is best adapted to the analysis called for? Trying to see the problem in perspective, 'as a rounded whole', will often settle this. Not even so big a subject may safely be studied in isolation. Britain was not the only participant, and Africa was not the only part of the world being parcelled out between European Powers at the same time. Thus it would be legitimate to compare British involvement with French and German motives; or the African process could be compared with that in the Pacific or with the threat of it in China. A moment's thought within these wider perspectives makes the adoption of a nearly-monocausal explanation look risky. Not that there has ever been any shortage of these, from J. A. Hobson's 'economic taproot' of powerful interests seeking to find markets for 'their surplus goods and their surplus capital' (1902) to Robinson and Gallagher's 'In the main British Africa was a gigantic [strategic] footnote to the Indian Empire' (1962).[4] If you decide to embark on a blistering critique of the latter dictum, there is no reason to suppose any university teacher will tear his hair out. But perhaps you will opt for the 'caravan'-type and will consider in turn all the possible explanations of British involvement: trading, strategic, philanthropic, political prestige or colonizing (in the strict sense of sending out white settlers); if you do, try to decide which should be given greatest weight, otherwise you may be accused of 'fence-sitting'.

In practice it is hard to think of a case within the extra-European field where a monocausal explanation could reasonably be employed. Anyone dealing with the Confederation of Canada in 1867 would, however, have to consider carefully whether such an explanation could be attempted. There are perhaps four main possible reasons why this Confederation was established. First, the unworkability of the existing constitutional system, the existence of problems incapable of solution within it and resultant ministerial political deadlock. Secondly, the desirability of expanding the economic base of Canada, and even more narrowly, perhaps, of finding a solution to the financial problems of the Grand Trunk Railway. Thirdly, imperial pressure for disengagement, to relieve Britain of the costs and anxieties of defending the Canadian colonies. Finally, fear of the United States. If the North lost the Civil War (1861–5), she might seek a compensating victory elsewhere; if she won, she might in her triumph emerge powerful, truculent and expansionist; and in either event Canada would be the obvious object of attack. The North had created the most powerful army in the world, a terrifying war-machine. It may well be, then, that fear of the United States *alone* could have led the Canadians to seek greater strength in unity. All Canadians wished to preserve their identity; and the Roman Catholic French Canadians in particular had no love for Protestant, Republican and materialistic Americans.

There are few problems which, with a modicum of preparation, cannot be quite adequately analysed in eight sections or fewer. One of the commonest mistakes made by undergraduates is to try to write an essay as if it were a book. As a corrective to this kind of leisurely narrative ramble, it is valuable to try the following exercise: formulate in one sentence a summary statement of, for example, what caused the Partition of Africa, and then expand an essay upwards on this base, making a concise explanation in eight paragraphs within your chosen structural framework. This is not meant as a call for a Chinese strait-jacket, but to suggest a simple way of laying an essay's foundations and building up its walls.

A building cannot be put up without scaffolding, but when it is finished, the scaffolding is removed. So it should be with the short essay. The cruder sign-posts of the plan should be eliminated. The frequent recurrence of phrases like 'as we shall see in a moment' or 'as I showed in the previous paragraph' are tedious to a reader and ought to be superfluous. The structural shape ideally should be clear enough to speak for itself. In matters of style, simplicity, clarity and conciseness are primary virtues, and purple passages should be avoided like the plague.

III

At this point, in case I am making the whole business seem more difficult than it is, I had best offer some words of encouragement. An undergraduate essay should be regarded as a legitimate literary form in its own right, and not as an interim substitute for the real article. We shall not all, it is true, as it is said Professor Trevor-Roper has done, one day be able to publish our undergraduate essays, nor is it given to most of us to equal the feat of the economist Professor Austin Robinson, who first worked out an ingenious methodological device in an answer written in an examination.[5] But serious history is a game which can be played by anyone who is willing to do some fairly intensive reading. Moreover, provided mere assertion is not mistaken for actual proof, to be 'good' one does not have to be 'right'. Better to have your own viewpoint, cogently presented but still capable of being shot down, than to stick cautiously to the apparently received version, which you may then find can be shot down too. Many of the best-known history books are 'wrong' in the sense that the interpretations they advance are not generally accepted. A classic case of the brilliantly 'wrong' book is Professor Ronald Robinson's and Professor Jack Gallagher's eminently readable *Africa and the Victorians* (1961), the theme of which is that the Partition of Africa was largely a strategically-dominated response to local nationalist challenges (from Egypt to South Africa) to European intervention. Again, the apprentice historian need not feel that he cannot wrestle with the supposed giants or act as umpire between experts who disagree. Finally he should not feel too inexperienced to interpret human behaviour.

These last two points are worth elaborating. As to competing with the professionals, the undergraduate has two assets which intermittently desert the mature practitioner: common sense and detachment. Common sense is something which everybody possesses. It is just a question of making sure it is developed and used. If a warning red light flashes the message 'this is nonsense' in front of your eyes, do not ignore it just because the author of the book you are reading is a well-known historian. His fame does not ensure him against becoming sometimes so involved with his sources that they come to dominate his whole horizon. Common sense often functions best when one is not too deeply involved.

The second big asset of the undergraduate is detachment. It is not he who has spent the best five years of his life in the dreary surroundings of the Public Record Office pencilling transcriptions of documents. It is not he who has succumbed to the temptation of squeezing out of his card-index an interpretation which is just a fraction larger than life, in order to stimulate a bit of healthy controversy through a dazzling sub-title, discerning yet another vital 'revolution' where his poor predecessors had seen only a row of beans. Thus the undergraduate is singularly well placed not only to see the wood rather than the trees but also to spot the bee in the bonnet. In some ways the physical (as well as the emotional) detachment from the documents actually puts the pre-research practitioner at an advantage. Historians ought always to penetrate behind the documents; instead many simply take their stand upon them. An historian using the cryptic British Cabinet minutes since 1917 probably would not make this mistake, but the historian most at risk is he who works in a field where the documents are rich and abundant, because he is tempted to think they will yield all the answers.

The very real advantage the undergraduate possesses can be illustrated by a comparison with the problems of a research worker engaged (say) in investigating British colonial policy in the period after the First World War, 1918–23. The materials are straightforwardly and accessibly arranged. But the quantity is daunting. The Colonial Office evidence alone consists (at a rough computation) of just under half-a-million files, many of them containing dozens of pages of foolscap. In addition, there are the files of other relevant government departments, the Cabinet records, the private papers of the leading ministers, parliamentary blue books and debates. An attempt to discover some of the possible pressures on policy-making will plunge the historian into newspapers, journals, and mission society records; and then he may wish to visit archives overseas. And so it goes on. He simply *cannot* even look at all the available evidence: it would take him a lifetime. As Miss Behrens has pointed out, trenchantly criticizing part of the argument of Professor Elton's *The Practice of History*,[6] it is a complete delusion in such circumstances to suppose 'that any given body of material would suggest all the concepts necessary to interpret it'; it is impossible to ask only such questions as arise *out* of the evidence, since no one will ever discover what all the evidence is. Thus all the historian can do in these circumstances is to put questions of his own choosing to a part of the evidence. Now the undergraduate knows this has to be so as far as he is concerned, although he sometimes imagines that if he could work with real documents he could evolve a more objective approach. This is improbable. The difference between himself and the professional historian (though the latter does not always admit it) is not one of kind but of degree; and as far as the difference in degree is concerned, the undergraduate has the better deal in many ways. He is, by his very divorce from the original documents and by using his common sense, sometimes more likely than the research historian to ask the really significant questions. Whilst articles in a learned journal dispute why people voted the way they did in the referenda on Australian federation in 1898–1900, the undergraduate is often quick to see this debate for the boring, inconclusive and unimportant thing it is, and proceed instead to ask why it was that the question of federation had become the subject of referenda at all, since this is an unusual feature in the history of federal schemes.

Nor need the undergraduate feel it impossible to discover what greater men than he have thought. Dr Steinberg offers a salutary 'law of history' in his contribution to this volume: 'We are no smarter than our ancestors'.[7] It is profoundly important always to remember this – without being deflated by it. But a rider might be added: 'Sometimes *they* were no smarter than *we* are.' This is, I think, the case surprisingly often, since not all rulers have the mind of a Metternich, and it is increasingly true as we reach contemporary history. The fumblings of today's rulers are notorious, and the decline of ability in statesmen is one of the most striking facts of the twentieth century. J. A. Spender, a most astute Edwardian journalist with close political contacts, had this to say about politicians – and it is even truer today than when he wrote it: 'The motives of politicians are few and simple, and the action they will and must take in given circumstances can nearly always be deduced with certainty by those who know the rules of the game.'[8] A major reason for this is the constraint normally placed on people by the mere act of holding supreme power: there is remarkably little room for freedom of manoeuvre at the top of the greasy pole. It is extremely difficult for any incoming government or successor régime to reverse the policies initiated by their predecessors, especially where commitments to foreign allies are involved, but even at home the fulfilment of electoral promises is for similar reasons often practically impossible. One simple rule in interpreting the statements and motives of politicians, therefore, is never to place the slightest reliance upon anything said by men out of office. Chatham lied about his intentions when later attacking the terms of the Peace of Paris which ended the Seven Years War in 1763. Dr Kwame Nkrumah changed his mind, after becoming prime minister in 1951, on the desirability of the compulsory cutting down of the 'swollen shoot'-infected cocoa trees on which Ghana's economy depended, an action he had previously opposed. Another simple rule for evaluating policy-making is to remember that the difference between, say, a Youth Club committee meeting and a Cabinet meeting is more apparent than real. The same inconclusiveness may charaterize both, and is only masked by the studied evasiveness of the Cabinet secretary's minutes. Like any other group of a dozen or more people sitting round a table (a circumstance which unfailingly brings out the worst in everybody), Cabinet ministers often have confused discussions, especially when matters are brought up without notice. Trivial matters often generate the most heat, while serious issues can go through on the nod, because the majority is bored or preoccupied. Sometimes ministers doze off. Read Thomas Jones' *Whitehall Diary*, which provides an unofficial 'inside story' of the 1920s, for examples. Nor are Cabinet decisions necessarily based upon sophisticated reasoning. Cynics say there is nothing intellectual or rational in politics. They may be correct; at any rate many men of affairs would agree with them, especially since formal decisions are not always implemented.

Moreover, few politicians in the world today, any more than in the past, have had any formal training in statecraft, though they may have run country estates or factories or trade unions, or been prominent in the kind of institutions, associational groups and leisure societies, such as schools, churches, literary and debating societies, which most people have encountered before they are eighteen. It ought not therefore to be too difficult to catch something of their mental processes. Government is an extremely difficult task, perhaps the most difficult task there is, but it is not quite so esoteric as most of its practitioners would have us believe. At all events, in trying to understand ruling élites, let us start with the world around us, and its power-hungry inhabitants whom we have already met: it can yield startling insights if we will let it. Whatever historian worth his salt would not have been glad to write as Miss Betty Behrens did in the preface of her book *The Ancien Régime* (1967): 'The writer owes many debts of gratitude – some ... to Cambridge University and Newnham College (whose ways of proceeding have made certain aspects of the Ancien Régime intelligible which otherwise might not have been so)....'

IV

The young historian can, therefore, soon learn to feel confident in analysing motive. He will quickly get caught up in problems of causation, which have a peculiar fascination for historians. Thus in considering the structure of historical argument, the content which may partially determine the form of the essay, it is as well to work out a few basic principles for dealing with it.

It is often possible to distinguish different 'levels' of explanation in dealing with specific, cataclysmic events like the outbreak of wars and revolutions. By separating the evidence into two categories, it is often possible to determine the moments in time when a possibility became a probability and finally a certainty. This is a technique as old as history itself, but often forgotten. It began with Thucydides when he tried to explain the outbreak of the Peloponnesian War in 431 B.C. Thucydides distinguished between, at one level, a given situation within which *a* war was likely because of underlying differences between the contestants, and, at another level, the specific causes of complaint, the immediate triggering mechanism which led to the actual outbreak of *the* war between Athens and Sparta.[9] It might be added that a likely war is never an inevitable war. There are wars that have been confidently predicted but subsequently averted. In Victorian times, what happened to the war that never came between Canada and the United States, or between England and France, or with Russia over India? And where, after 1898, did the war which anybody would then have predicted, that between England and Germany, come from? Nevertheless, Thucydides' distinction remains extremely valuable, and there are far too many accounts of causation which concentrate on one level to the exclusion of the other. Even if they do not end up in untenable monocausality, they remain unconvincing. Dual levels always exist in the explanation of specific datable events, and may not be absent from the broader evolutionary processes either.

As an example, let us take the outbreak of the Anglo-Boer War in South Africa in 1899. Here, a variety of explanations confronts us. On the one side, General Jan Smuts denounced it from the Boer point of view as the culmination of a 'century of wrong' in British policy; on the other, Colonial Secretary Joe Chamberlain declared it was a just and necessary attempt to strengthen the 'weakest link in the Imperial chain'. One historian states that the 'discovery of gold on the Witwatersrand led to war between Britain and the Boer republics'. Another says that the chain of events leading to war started *before* gold was discovered in 1885 because Gladstone had already in effect 'abdicated to Kruger'. Yet another explains it in terms of the intolerable grievances endured by the Uitlanders, the unenfranchised Transvaal British mining community. Others see it explicitly in terms of personal antagonism: 'Joe's War' in some cases, 'Milner's War' in others, both meeting President Kruger's 'intransigence'. Others consider it in terms of vague impersonal forces – a manifestation of 'the high tide of imperialism'. To sort out this confusion, start by eliminating the useless explanations, such as 'Milner's War' or 'the high tide of imperialism': the Anglo-Boer War was, like any other war, a conflict between state interests and ideologies, not a contest between individuals or abstractions. Next, distinguish between points of detail and the broader issues: High Commissioner Milner's plea for 'enfranchisement for the

Uitlanders' is clearly not on the same level of explanation as his pronouncement about 'the great game . . . for the mastery of South Africa'. Then, having distinguished the levels of explanation, decide whether to jettison resort to monocausality of the 'no gold, no war' type. Gold *may* have created a situation within which a possible war became more likely, but it did not enable President Kruger to pursue his main aims, such as an outlet to the sea, any the more effectively, and it clearly was not the *casus belli*.[10] Finally, it is worth pausing to ask exactly what one is left with. Is there an averted war to consider? Why didn't the war break out earlier? Why was escalation contained? Why didn't the African majority exploit the opportunity of rising against their divided white masters? Such hypothetical questions put us on the track of an important point which would otherwise be overlooked – that a precondition of the Anglo-Boer War was the decline in Bantu vital force from the 1880s. Only with this precondition could the white community afford the luxury of war. It is significant that both sides preferred to run the risk of losing it rather than mobilize Africans on their side. What the French and English had done with the Amer-Indians in the struggle for mastery in America in the eighteenth century, the British and Boers would have found inconceivable in nineteenth-century South Africa.

Now for a couple of warnings about methods of argument. One of the most deadly traps is that diagnosed as *post hoc* [*ergo*] *propter hoc*. This is simply the fallacy of confusing consequence with sequence. Because a course of action was advocated before an event, the event itself, with hindsight, appears to have been caused by the advocacy. The role of coincidence is too easily overlooked. For example, in 1839 Lord Durham, in a famous *Report on the Affairs of British North America*, advocated a union of the French and British provinces of Canada and also colonial responsible self-government. In 1840 the Canadas were united and in 1849 the Canadians obtained virtual responsible government. Historians have therefore long argued that the decisions of 1840 and 1849 may be seen as the implementation of Lord Durham's recommendations. From this it is but a short step to the elevation of the Durham Report into one of the head corner-stones of the modern Commonwealth. Only very recently has it occurred to anyone to ask whether this explanation falls within the category of a *post hoc propter hoc* argument. Mr Ged Martin has suggested that there is good reason to believe that far from the Report's persuading the British Government to unite the Canadas it was an embarrassment to them, since they had decided for other reasons to adopt the policy, and Lord Durham had so disgraced himself by his ludicrous ostentation and arrogance that he was not taken seriously by them or anyone else. Nor is the connection between Durham's views on self-government and what was actually introduced a decade later any closer. The connection has always been cemented with reference to the fact that in 1849 the colonial secretary was Durham's brother-in-law and the governor-general his son-in-law; but Durham regularly disagreed with the former and never lived to meet the latter.[11]

Another example of the quite exceptionally insidious nature of this *post hoc propter hoc* trap is provided by Africa. Some tribal kings and chiefs in the nineteenth century abolished circumcision, or, more rarely, bridewealth payments or polygyny, which missionaries had consistently urged them to do. When some chiefs took such a decision to abolish, the missionaries automatically assumed it was the direct result of their own pressure. Sometimes they mistook suspension for abolition. That there might have been good indigenous reasons seldom occurred to them; and African rulers, like most practical politicians, saw no reason to stop the missionaries believing what they wanted to believe if this kept them happy. The historian has to probe a little deeper, however. The trouble about initiation ceremonies involving circumcision was that they seriously reduced the availability of young men for warfare, and it was this which led warlike states to drop them.

Another trap to be avoided in analysing causation is in essence a semantic one. It is the resort to abstract 'isms'; worse still, the use of vogue words to explain one vague phenomenon in terms of another equally vague phenomenon. Other contributors to this volume have dwelt on the dangers of 'isms', so there is no need to say much about them here. It was the proudest boast of one of England's best historians in recent times, the late Professor T. S. Ashton, that with the single non-contentious exception of 'baptism' he had written an entire text-book on English economic history in the eighteenth century without ever once resorting to a word ending in 'ism'. (He also contrived to use the shorthand term 'Industrial Revolution' only once in the book.) History would be written a lot better if everybody applied Ashton's principle to their own work.[12]

V

Terminological caution of this kind is especially desirable in the field of extra-European history, since the phrases 'western imperialism', 'neo-colonialism' and so forth not only contain all the normal hazards of 'ism' words, but also have two added difficulties. They are rather hard to avoid using; they have also become loaded with emotive and polemical overtones. You have got to be very clever indeed to get away with a dictum such as 'Nationalism is the continuation of Imperialism by other means'; in its context it *has* a verifiable meaning, but only because it uses the words in ways which are not self-evidently obvious.[13] 'New nationalism is old tribalism writ large' is a deplorable example of the tendency to think one 'ism' can be explained in terms of another. It may point towards a truth, but it is certainly not an ideal way of formulating the truth about Africa in the twentieth century.

Thus, although much of what I have written so far applies to most areas of history, it is plain that the extra-European field has its own special pitfalls. Chief among these is the risk of over-facile generalization, of which the importing of useless 'isms' into the analyses of causation is a symptom. But there are others too.

If your study is of the 'Expansion of Europe', defined as the political, economic and cultural relations between Europeans and non-Europeans, you have a formidable task. It calls forth every art from that of intercontinental gymnastics to skating on thin ice. It requires a certain amount of agility to compare developments in China, Latin America and the Middle East, or to hop between India and Africa, or to become equally at home in the history of Ireland and Australia, or to contrast the economic development of China, Japan, Turkey and Brazil, or to compare the reasons for the breakdown of the Central African Federation with those of the West Indies and

Malaysia. Yet all these feats can be performed successfully.[14] The motives of all European powers, and their methods of ruling empires, were not necessarily identical, though there are basic similarities. Non-European responses were not uniform. When one embarks upon the challenging assignment of analysing these differences, the main problem is to avoid being intimidated by the plethora of unmasterable facts. This is where some methodological guide-lines about causation, however crude, are essential, and where a rigorous structural framework can encourage a habit of ruthless selectivity and check a tendency to become confused by imperfect acquaintance with the detailed sequence of events. It is great fun skating on thin ice, but very dangerous unless one knows where the really weak spots are. In a vast subject like the Expansion of Europe it is often impossible to avoid a high level of generalization which is not backed by a knowledge of the history of individual countries as complete and as detailed as historians of Europe take for granted, but there are nevertheless places where this sort of generalization would be unacceptably superficial. It is vital to realize where extreme precision of detail is essential, where the corners cannot be turned too sharply, or the movement flurried.

Almost by definition the Expansion of Europe contains a central core of awkward questions where glib generalization will not do. They occur mainly at the junction points of Western influences and African and Asian responses. The precise nature of the pressures and their effect has to be carefully determined. This type of enquiry has been bedevilled in many cases because tender European consciences have been prone to exaggerate the disintegrating effect of Western influences (though there is also an opposite group of cases where the reverse is true; unfortunately there is not room to discuss these here). Those who campaigned for the abolition of the slave trade (achieved in 1807) argued that pressure on West African societies to supply slaves for the West Indian sugar plantations was responsible for fomenting wars in Yorubaland and turning the hinterland of Dahomey and Lagos into a sea of blood. The reply to this could be that the Europeans did not bring either slave-raiding or warfare to West Africa, that all was not sweetness and light before the white man arrived, and that African wars, like wars anywhere else, had political causes of their own. A reply would also have to try to establish how deeply into the interior the catchment area for slaves extended.[15] The history of Egypt provides a variation on the same theme. Muhammad 'Ali (1806–49) was a notable ruler who made a vigorous effort to diversify the Egyptian economy, including an unsuccessful attempt to establish factories for the manufacture of cotton goods. Did Muhammad 'Ali fail because his policies were unrealistic and his administration incompetent, or because Britain under Palmerston was determined to thwart him in order to keep and expand Egypt as a primary producer of raw cotton for the mills of Lancashire?[16]

Then, to take an even more important and difficult example, there are the guilty European or accusing Chinese fingers pointing to a connection between the so-called Opium War (the first Anglo-Chinese War of 1839–42) and the outbreak of the Taiping Rebellion or Revolution (1850–64), which, in terms of size, duration, and destructiveness, was probably the biggest single event known to Europeans in the nineteenth century. The Taiping Rebellion began in the hinterland of Canton, the major port for European trading on the China coast. It is probably impossible to deny all connection between Western influences and the Taiping Rebellion, particularly in view of the third-hand pseudo-Christianity of its ideology. But its exact nature needs careful formulation. Further, one must not forget the underlying population explosion in China which preceded it and might have caused it anyway. Between 1766 and 1833 the Chinese population grew from approximately 208 million to 399 million, while the area of cultivated land remained to all intents and purposes the same. Equally one must not lose sight of the fact that other huge rebellions were concurrently taking place deep in the Chinese interior. Two of these both lasted from 1855 to 1873. Another, and perhaps just as significant a rebellion as the Taiping itself, was the Nien rebellion (1850–68), and this too appears to have been nearly unrelated to Western influences. Only fifteen years ago, the Taiping Rebellion was almost unheard of in the west, while the relatively trivial Boxer Rebellion of 1898 was known because it was so obviously related to the Manchu desire to turn out the 'foreign devils'. Attention is now becoming focused more closely upon the indigenous reasons for the collapse of Manchu rule, and Western pressures on the coast might come to be regarded as aggravations only. Be that as it may, there was clearly something in the sociology of China which seems almost automatically to have produced massive turbulence.[17]

These three examples of problems, which partly involve trying to measure the extent of disintegration in West Africa, Eygpt and China for which the West may be 'blamed', all represent points of controversy where the crux of an argument must be formed without moralizing self-righteousness, but after a thorough appraisal of the alternatives. In Indian history a similar question emerges: did Britain practise 'divide and rule' over Muslims and Hindus, or did these two religious communities divide themselves – or does the truth lie somewhere in between? In presenting your own conclusion to such questions, don't smooth out the complexity or drain away all evidence of the tortured effort through which you have arrived at an opinion.

It follows that in order to answer difficult but critical problems about the role of the West in world history it is essential to acquire some ability, however rudimentary, to establish the differences in social structure and intellectual outlook between Europe and, for example, Confucian China and the Islamic states which stretch from Morocco to Malaya. It is also fascinating to be able to discern how far traditional ways of life and thought have been carried over into the 'colonial era' and transmuted by it. Again, does Mao Tse-tung owe more to the Taiping leader Hung Hsiu-ch'uan or to Karl Marx?

The young Western historian may wonder whether it is in fact possible to understand an alien society at all. His detachment may give insights but it could also act as a barrier. The outsider is perhaps uniquely qualified to understand societies *relatively* like his own and to penetrate their myths and realities. Consider for example the astonishing insight which various Frenchmen have attained into the working of democracies in other countries: Alexis de Tocqueville for America (1835), André Siegfried for New Zealand (1914) and Elie Halévy for England (1912–32). It was, however, an Englishman, J. E. C. Bodley (in his book *France*, 1907) who saw the

French better than they could see themselves. So far so good. But how shall Western historians fathom societies quite unlike their own? It is hard enough sometimes to understand even some 'European' off-shoot societies, such as South Africa's Afrikanerdom, though the attempt is in this case eased a little by pondering the parallel with Sparta holding down the helots, or Prussia confronting the Slavs: all three are examples of communities feeling themselves to be superior to, but threatened by, a numerically larger, alien population: and in each case the dominant minorities developed authoritarian, intransigent and militaristic attitudes. It is harder still to penetrate the mentality of the Nuer of the Sudan. Hardest of all, perhaps, is the difficulty experienced in the West of understanding China. Yet the effort has got to be made to penetrate behind the clichés about 'inscrutable Orientals' or 'the Confucian ethic'. J. K. Fairbank's *The United States and China* (rev. ed., Cambridge, Mass., 1972) is a penetrating introduction. Elsewhere sociologists and anthropologists can help, and it's better to read first-rate anthropology than third-rate history. But sociologists are apt to rely excessively on 'models' and anthropologists, traditionally at least, on static description, to which the historian has to add his distinctive concern for a time-scale and his flexible feeling for change.

Some weeks after this chapter was drafted, I had to mark some examination papers in African history. I did not enjoy the task, chiefly because I found much of the writing too abstract, and I had a strong feeling that in many cases the candidates themselves did not really understand the jargon they were using. They seemed often to be merely mouthing fashionable catch-phrases and sociological clichés. I reproduce here some of their descriptions of the processes of change in modern African societies, because they illustrate the danger of cloaking the understanding of individual cases by undefined jargon and wordy abstraction.

'Nineteenth-century generalized intra-élite fissiparity and institutionalized internal fission did not prevent the Basuto from emerging in the twentieth century as a socio-political entity.' 'After independence, this syncretic society had an asymmetry of institutions.' 'Colonial nationalism in each territory was the product of a range of variables, many of which were exogenous stimuli.' 'Through a discontinuous process of political socialization there has been a transition from an organic, ascriptive society to a large, differentiated and meritocratic society in which institutions develop their own autonomous goals.' 'We can observe a ready politicization of urban-dwellers into consensus opposition.' 'Peasant actions were objectively revolutionary but subjectively they were not.' 'Models of instability show that quasi-proletarianization and the "revolution of rising expectations" leads to institutioned [*sic*] military coup [*sic*] by "grass-roots" military men.'

Now you may think that it is unfair to rip statements out of context and expect them to be readily intelligible. I would reject that defence. We are writing history, telling a story, and not analysing abstract phenomena. I would not like to say that all of these examples are inaccurate, still less bad sociology, but they are certainly unattractive, and queer history. Some, clearly, are as bogus as they are sentimental, excusable only in as much as they are genuine attempts to grapple with difficult problems in a way suggested by excellent teachers of the subject (who would be horrified to see some of the travesties of what they thought they had described to their pupils). Too many historians write about African history in a sociological way designed to make it seem a sophisticated study of sophisticated peoples. Reactions against Trevor-Roper, Col Blimp and Government White Papers can go too far. The Mau Mau movement in Kenya in the 1950s, whatever else it was (peasant revolt, Kikuyu civil war, savage anti-European rising), cannot be summed up and white-washed simply (or rather, not so simply) as a 'nationalist politicisation and mobilisation of the Kikuyu people . . . an integral part of an ongoing, rationally-conceived nationalist movement' (C. J. Rosberg and J. Nottingham, *The Myth of 'Mau Mau'*, 1966, xvii). It is a disservice to Africans to write their history in this sloppy way. It is also a disservice to African history to use a special jargon to describe it, since this only serves to reinforce the nonsensical notion that it is fundamentally different from (and inferior to) European history, the writing of which has got along well enough until recently without pseudo-sociological abominations. May I repeat: the sociologists' concepts can be illuminating starting-points and useful tools of historical study, but only if they are thoroughly understood, related to actual events, freed from emotional bias, and clearly expressed.

VI

By now, I hope I can assume that the reader feels reasonably happy about structure and method: 'how to write an essay.' Genuine intellectual content must be put into it, otherwise the worst features of the stereotyped 'eight-legged essay' will proliferate. An interpretation, a theme, must be thought out. Winston Churchill once crushingly remarked of a rather floppy-looking pudding that it 'lacked a theme'. If even a pudding needs a theme, how much more does an essay.

As far as extra-European history is concerned, the theme cannot be one seen simply through European eyes. The content of an essay cannot be Eurocentric if it is to give anything like half the answer. Most countries in the last century and a half have been subjected to Western influences, but they did not all respond in the same way. Partly this was because the form in which they experienced Western influence varied: much of India and Africa were painted red on the map, while China and Latin America, also objects of attention, were not. It is interesting to discover why this was. In any event, the obvious larger variable in the cultural equation is on the non-European side, and for this reason, extra-European studies must be coloured by trying to see the problem of interaction from within the African or Asian communities.

Professor Owen Lattimore has urged the necessity for this kind of reorientation with much cogency: to 'cultivate an intellectual method of seeing China from within and looking from China outward at the world'. He goes on to explain how to the West the five Treaty Ports established in 1842 were designed to create centres of law and order. But, he adds, with great precision, 'from the Chinese point of view, the Treaty Ports, symbols of law and order and security for investments which the foreign powers kept pressing successive Chinese governments to promote, were in fact centres of infection poisoning law and order and spreading insecurity into China' – a view which was vindicated during the present century when the

Japanese used Treaty Ports like Shanghai and Tientsin as beach-heads for the invasion of China, and the other Treaty Powers stood impotently by. The extra-territorial privileges and jurisdiction the Ports accorded to Westerners came to cover their Chinese employees as well, and this was not healthy for Chinese stability or for the loyalty of Chinese to their own government.[18]

This attempt to see other societies 'from within looking outward' provides a most exciting extension of perspective which the parochial study of England or Europe alone can seldom do to quite the same extent. What (to amend Kipling) should they know of English history who only English history know? Ventures into extra-European history force a modification, for example, of the Western historian's concept of religion. It is not simply that the strictly theocratic nature of Muslim states has to grasped (since Islam does not distinguish Church from state and has no specific priesthood). It is also a question of looking at African and other religions more as an anthropologist does, in a broader context that that of an ethical or theological system, and of seeing them in their social contexts as unifying agencies and as means of explaining and coping with the sources of misfortune in life.

Every part of the world has its features so fundamental that they often become overlooked. There have been historical essays on Irish history which never mentioned religion and some on India which never mentioned caste. The story of the Indian nationalist movement, in a sub-continent with at least 179 main languages and 544 dialects, has to trace the relationship between the decisions of the 1830s to make English the language of education and government and the emergence of a new élite suckled on this 'milk of the tigress', as Tilak called it. Differences in Muslim and Hindu reaction have to be elucidated. What better guide in these matters than Dr Seal's book?[19] By considering the context within which English education took place, one can see why the singing of hymns about prisoners leaping to loose their chains (or Nehru's reading of Trevelyan's *Garibaldi* trilogy) affected Indian schoolboys completely differently from the way in which they affected (or more probably didn't affect) English schoolboys. One sees the impact in law courts and the emergence of the lawyer–politician. It is often said that British ineptitude in handling nationalist movements stems from the fact that she herself has not in modern history experienced alien rule. The historian, however, has to imagine what it is like.

Looking at Africa from the inside, the historian tries to understand the implications of living in small-scale, pre-literate, polygynous and perhaps 'stateless' (acephalous) communities. He adjusts himself to viewing marriage as a contract between kin-groups rather than between romantically involved individuals, and, for pastoral peoples, to thinking in terms of 'wives and other cattle'. Among many other shifts from Western viewpoints, he tries, for instance, to understand the incalculable importance attached to the possession of cattle for social, ritual, political, and aesthetic reasons: cattle are a measure of status, a means of mediation with ancestor spirits, and a necessity for ratifying marriage. Amongst many African peoples too, land was traditionally viewed as a commodity to be enjoyed in common, which, no more than the air we breathe, could be the subject of unilaterally alienable private property: dead ancestors had rights in it, and although chiefs might convey rights of *use* and obligations of responsibility to individuals, this was still not quite the same notion as Western ideas of property rights.[20] Only with these facts in mind is it possible to understand the full significance for Africans of the alienation of land to Europeans or the 1890s rinderpest epidemics, or, in the twentieth century, of land-apportionment and rehabilitation schemes, or of veterinary embargoes or government destocking programmes.

VII

None of these shifts of attitude necessarily poses harder intellectual problems than those involved in understanding medieval Christendom or, for public schoolboys, English working-class sub-culture. Moreover, as inter-continental comparisons are built up, so the situation in one part of the world throws fruitful light upon what happened, or did not happen, in other parts. And no one plunges completely naked into the bracing waters of extra-European history. Existing knowledge of the better-traversed areas of Greek and Roman, or Tudor and Stuart, history are helpful starting-points. It is noteworthy that Ronald Syme, Professor of Ancient History, has published lectures on *Colonial Élites: Rome, Spain and the Americas* (1958).

There is a notorious Eurocentric pronouncement by Professor Trevor-Roper to the effect that we cannot afford to 'amuse ourselves with the unrewarding gyrations of barbarous tribes in picturesque but irrelevant corners of the globe'.[21] The history of Merovingian kings and Buganda kabakas is however not dissimilar in its gyrations; and in terms of purely military achievements and growing megalomania Shaka Zulu between 1818 and 1828 can be compared with Alexander the Great. The preoccupations of African leaders or Chinese scholar-officials in the nineteenth century were similar to their sixteenth- and seventeenth-century European counterparts, and in some respects to their contemporary counterparts too. The gradual resolution of tensions between centre and periphery, as consolidating and unitary state-building processes proceed (or recede), the reduction (or growth) of regional autonomies and peripheral provincial resistances: these form part and parcel of the history of every major country in the world, of Mughal India and Maoist China as well as medieval France and modern Germany. He who has studied what Julius Caesar did for the Roman Republic, or Henry II for the Angevin empire, or the early Tudors for Britain – rescuing states from overmighty subjects, lack of governance and bureaucratic breakdown, local war-lords and internecine conflicts within ruling élites, and then reconstituting popular allegiance and administrative machinery – will be admirably placed to measure the achievement of Moshweshwe in re-creating and holding together nineteenth-century Lesotho, or Mao Tse-tung in bringing some order out of chaos in twentieth-century China, because he understands how in these circumstances government becomes of necessity a personal *tour de force*. He will also have come to expect that the efforts of these leaders will be jeopardized after their death if crucial problems of succession are not resolved.[22] The ways in which more impersonal bureaucracies emerge are not totally dissimilar in England and in Asante.[23] Techniques of warding off external attack have wide similarities throughout the world. Sparta in sixth-century

Greece avoided fighting in much the same way as Dahomey in nineteenth-century West Africa, both achieving immunity from attack through manipulating a range of propaganda weapons which cumulatively created an impression of terrifying invincibility. While Sparta manipulated the Delphic Oracle, Dahomey contrived to frighten off Europeans by deliberately exaggerating the extent of its 'cannibalism'.[24] Conspicuous largesse and hospitality as the test of rank and the most admired virtue among leading squires and nobles in sixteenth- and early seventeenth-century England reflect exactly the attributes expected of the chief of an African tribe.[25] Many pages of E. P. Thompson's *Making of the English Working Class* deal with the kind of millenarian expectations which have been so widespread in recent African history, and in particular his treatment of Joanna Southcott of Devonshire (*c.* 1800) forms an ideal prelude to studying the upheavals caused by African prophetesses from Nongqause in Xhosaland in 1857 to Alice Lenshina a hundred years later in Zambia.[26] As far as economic history is concerned, Professor R. L. Heilbroner's *The Making of Economic Society* (1962) serves at least as well as an introductory text-book for African history as it does for the pre-industrial history of Europe before the eighteenth century. I hasten to add that I do not mean to suggest that any of these particular parallels must be made, are genuinely close, or that they would repay serious study. Nor do I urge that these books should be read if you have not already read them. I merely use them to illustrate the general point that whatever you have read can provide a genuine starting-point for approaching extra-European history.

So too with the study of the means by which European imperial powers held a whole world under their control in the nineteenth century: understanding this is not so difficult a problem as at first it might appear. Hans Christian Andersen's story of the Emperor's new clothes, or George Orwell's account of *Shooting an Elephant* in Burma (1936) go a long way towards explaining not only how a few score Europeans held millions in thrall simply by projecting the idea of their own unquestionable omniscience and effortless superiority, but also how nationalist reaction set in when peoples woke up to the fact that the emperor indeed had no clothes and that a white man's skull under his pith sun-helmet was as thin as anybody else's. The imperial guardians were mainly amateurs who proceeded from the known (including Greek and Roman history) to the unknown. Lord Palmerston worked pragmatically on the simple homely principle that looking after world-wide British interests was only a problem of estate-management writ large, and the principle served him well enough in the circumstances of his time. For Victorian aristocrats the same great unwashed scum stretched from Bermondsey to Bangkok. When Harry East went east from Rugby School, his chum Tom Brown had no doubt that he would do well in the Indian Army, since 'No fellow could handle boys better, and I suppose [native] soldiers are very like boys.' Lord Lugard's *Memoranda* on Nigerian government, 'Indirect Rule', and his *Dual Mandate in British Tropical Africa* may look daunting and technical, but every schoolboy or boy-scout can grasp the fundamental message. Lugard hoped that the Muslim emirs of Northern Nigeria would be taught 'to acquire an English schoolboy's ideas of honour, loyalty and above all responsibility'. They were to be his prefects or patrol-leaders. Like Indian princes they became fine cricketers and polo-players. British governors all over the world saw to it that the natives were encouraged to play football and cricket, since, as one of them put it 'a similarity of taste in amusements is a guarantee for common sympathy in more important matters'. The whole subject of imperial control is being studied more seriously these days, after the pioneering efforts of Professor Anthony Low, whose stimulating book *Lion Rampant* ought to be widely read.[27]

The British have always relied heavily on analogy. This is a fact which makes the study of their behaviour on the world stage reasonably easy as well as peculiarly fascinating. During the eighteenth and nineteenth centuries, the family metaphor was repeatedly applied to all discussions of relations between the 'mother country' and her 'daughter colonies'. The analogy of the Canadian constitutional solution of 1867 was applied in an attempt to solve the problems of governing South Africa in 1906–10. The American constitution stood as a perpetual challenge and left its mark on Australia from 1900. The 'federal panacea' was a concept used as a means of re-asserting imperial control as well as a device for decolonization. Pre-1914 federal white colonial devolutions were hopefully applied to Indian constitutional planning in the 1930s and to Central Africa, the West Indies, Malaysia and elsewhere in the 1950s. Such use of analogy frequently proved to be unfortunate in its results. Mid-nineteenth-century Indian experience influenced policy for the new tropical African acquisitions from the 1880s, being first refined through Lord Cromer's Egyptian administration (1883–1907). The historian is sceptical of the supposed lessons of history, and he quickly learns the dangers of dependence on analogy: its use to him is mostly as an initial guide-line in tackling unfamiliar problems. But the fact remains that politicians (like clergymen in their sermons) have always relied on it fundamentally and show no signs of ceasing to do so. They have an unhappy knack of often seizing upon the wrong analogy. The apotheosis of this disastrous tendency was reached in the Suez Crisis of 1956 during the premiership of Sir Anthony Eden. Eden later unrepentantly described the theme of his memoirs as 'the lessons of the thirties and their application to the fifties'. He did not seem to realize that much had changed in the meantime and that in any case the correct analogue for Colonel Ab'dul Nasser in the 1950s was not Adolf Hitler in the 1930s, but Arabi Pasha in the 1880s.[28]

VIII

In conclusion, there are three points which I would like to underline. First, since the history essay is a respectable form of literary composition in its own right, its content deserves to be cast in a properly considered structural framework. The importance of thinking out an interpretative theme, and planning its presentation, is especially important in the large areas of extra-European history if coherent units of study are to emerge. Second, whilst not denying that extra-European history presents a considerable challenge to a beginner, I hope I have indicated that it is possible to devise straightforward methodological tactics for coping with this challenge. Even where these involve drawing upon the findings of sociologists and anthropologists, or looking outward from within Asian and African societies, the exercise is not different in kind from that encountered in more traditional historical studies: to comprehend difference and measure change and account for it. A small town grammar school and a world-wide empire present similar problems in historical reconstruction; and this is a fact which not only assists the study of extra-European history, but may also be fed back to attain a fuller and refreshed understanding of European, English and local history.[29] Lastly, there is no such thing as finality in historical explanation, and thus there is no theory or interpretation which may not one day be revised or even disproved totally. New evidence does not necessarily have to come to light for this to happen. The process is almost invariably started by some quite modest thought, by exercising a bit of common sense and adopting a fresh angle of vision. Young or old, the historian can develop a rigorously critical spirit which takes nothing on trust (and denies itself the benefit of the doubt), and he can attempt to see, evaluate and write about a problem historically as 'a rounded whole'. In so doing he will edge a little nearer the truth.

Notes:

1. J. R. Levenson, *Confucian China and its modern fate* (1958), I, p. 43.
2. The terms 'citadel' and 'caravan' are borrowed from the title of an essay (comparing the British and American 'Establishments') by F. Thistlethwaite in *American Quarterly*, 40 (1957).
3. For some interesting reflections on this theme see F. H. Hinsley, *Power and the pursuit of peace* (1963).
4. J. A. Hobson, *Imperialism, a study* (1902), pp. 105–6; R. E. Robinson and J. Gallagher, 'The Partition of Africa' in *New Cambridge Modern History* (1962), XI, p. 616.
5. H. R. Trevor-Roper, *Historical Essays* (1957); Joan Robinson, *The Economics of Imperfect Competition* (1965 ed.), p. 163 and note.
6. B. Behrens, in a review in *Historical Journal* 12 (1969), pp. 190–3.
7. Above, p. 60.

8. J. A. Spender, *Life, Journalism and Politics* (1927), I, p. 113.
9. Thucydides, *The Peloponnesian War* I. xxiii/6 or p. 25 in the Penguin Classics translation.
10. Compare J. S. Marais, *The Fall of Kruger's Republic* (1961); D M. Schreuder, *Gladstone and Kruger . . . 1880–85* (1969); G. H. Le May, *British Supremacy in South Africa 1899–1907* (1965) and *The Oxford History of South Africa* II *1870–1966* (1971, ed. M. Wilson and L. Thompson), pp. 313–33.
11. Ged Martin, *The Durham Report and British Policy: a critical essay* (1972).
12. T. S. Ashton, *An Economic History of England: the Eighteenth Century* (1955), p. vi and p. 125.
13. Robinson and Gallagher, in *New Cambridge Modern History* XI, p. 640.
14. See for example: N. Mansergh, *The Commonwealth Experience,* (1969); R. E. Robinson and J. Gallagher, *Africa and the Victorians* (1961) Ch. 1; D. C. M. Platt, "The Imperialism of Free Trade"[22]: some reservations', *Economic History Review,* 21 (1968); Professors J. A. Gallagher, D. A. Low and E. T. Stokes have all published monographs on African as well as Indian history. See also: S. Kuznets (ed.) *Economic Growth: Brazil, India and Japan* (1955) and R. E. Ward and D. A. Rustow (eds.) *Political Modernisation in Japan and Turkey* (Princeton N. J. 1964).
15. J. Gallagher, 'Economic Relations in Africa', in *New Cambridge Modern History* (1957), VII, p. 575 and R. E. Smith, in *Yoruba Warfare in the Nineteenth Century,* ed. J. F. A. Ajayi and R. E. Smith, (1964), p. 52.
16. Compare the 'anti-Muhammad 'Ali' view of H. A. B. Rivlin *The Agricultural Policy of Muhammad 'Ali in Egypt*. (Harvard 1961) with the older account by V. J. Puryear, *International Economics and Diplomacy in the Near East 1834–53* (Stanford 1935).
17. F. Michael, *The Taiping Rebellion* I (Washington UP Seattle 1966), pp. 15–19, S. Y. Teng, *The Taiping Rebellion and the Western Powers* (1971), pp. 21–24, 356, 391, Li Chien-nung, *The Political History of China 1840–1928* (tr. Teng and Ingalls, Princeton NJ 1956), pp. 51–2.
18. O. Lattimore, *From China Looking Outward* (1964).
19. A. Seal, *The Emergence of Indian Nationalism* (1968), especially 'The formation of the new élite' pp. 104–61.
20. The following may serve as suitable introductory reading for historians needing a basic grounding in anthropology: G.

Lienhardt, *Social Anthropology* (1964), or Lucy Mair, *An introduction to Social Anthropology* (1965); for Africa in particular, see M. Gluckman, *Politics, Law and Ritual in Tribal Society* (1965); Lucy Mair, *Primitive Government* (1962); E. E. Evans-Pritchard, *Witchcraft, Oracles and Magic among the Azande* (1937); Jomo Kenyatta, *Facing Mount Kenya* (1938); M. Fortes and E. E. Evans-Pritchard (eds.) *African Political Systems* (1940, 1963); A. R. Radcliffe-Brown & D. Forde (eds.) *African systems of kinship and marriage* (1950).

21. H. R. Trevor-Roper, *The Rise of Christian Europe* (1965), p. 9.
22. Compare for example: H. H. Scullard, *From the Gracchi to Nero* (2nd ed. 1963), pp. 148–58; J. Boussard, *Le Gouvernement d'Henri II Plantagenêt* (Paris 1956); G. R. Elton, *England under the Tudors* (1955); S. Schram, *Mao Tse-tung* (1966) and J. D. Omer-Cooper, *The Zulu Aftermath* (1966), pp. 99–114.
23. Compare G. R. Elton, *The Tudor Revolution in Government* (1953); Max Weber, *The Theory of Social and Economic Organisation* (tr. Henderson and Parsons, Glencoe, Illinois 1947), pp. 3, 324–407 and I. Wilks 'Aspects of Bureaucratisation in Ashanti' in *Journal of African History*, VII, (1966).
24. For similarities between Sparta and Dahomey, compare V. Ehrenberg 'A Totalitarian State' in *Aspects of the Ancient World* (1946) with ch. by J. Lombard, in *West African Kingdoms in the Nineteenth Century*, ed. D. Forde and P. M. Kaberry, (1967), pp. 71–91, and ch. by I. A. Akinjogbin, in *A thousand years of West African History*, ed. J. F. A. Ajayi and I. Espie (Ibadan 1965), pp. 309–26; R. F. Burton, *A Mission to Gelele, King of Dahomey* (*1864*), specifically called Dahomeans a 'breed of black Spartans' (I, p. 85).
25. Compare L. Stone, *The Crisis of the Aristocracy 1558–1641* (1965), p. 42 and R. H. Tawney, *Business and Politics under James I: Lionel Cranfield* (1958), pp. 141–2 with I. Schapera, *Government and Politics in tribal society* (1956, 1963), pp. 40–93.
26. Compare E. P. Thompson, *The Making of the English Working Class* (1963), especially pp. 382 ff, with E. Roux, *Time Longer than Rope: a history of the Black Man's struggle for freedom in South Africa* (1948), pp. 40–50 and ch. by A. D. Roberts, in *Protest and Power in Black Africa*, ed. R. Rotberg and A. Mazrui (1970), pp. 513–71; see also the 'Chronological Index of Scripture History, etc.' in John Brown's *Self-Interpreting Family Bible* (1st ed. Edinburgh 1778) for a prediction that the millennium would begin in 1866, or failing that in 2016.

27. H. C. Andersen, *Eventyr, fortalte for Børn,* I.3 'Keiserens nye Klaeder' (Copenhagen 1837); George Orwell, *Collected Essays, Journalism and Letters of...* (1968) I. pp. 235–42; Thomas Hughes, *Tom Brown's Schooldays* (1857), part 2, ch. viii; F. D. Lugard, *The Dual Mandate in British Tropical Africa* (4th ed. 1929); Hercules Robinson, *Speeches* (1879); D. A. Low, 'Lion Rampant', *Journal of Commonwealth Political Studies,* ii (1963/4). pp. 235–50, reprinted with other essays as *Lion Rampant* (1973).
28. *The Memoirs of Sir Anthony Eden:* II *Full Circle* (1960), foreword. T. Little, *Eygpt* (1958), pp. 210–12 and J. Marlowe, *Anglo-Egyptian Relations 1800–1953* (1954), p. 403 demonstrate the parallel between Nasser and Arabi Pasha.
29. Keith Thomas, *Religion and the Decline of Magic: studies in popular beliefs in sixteenth and seventeenth century England* (1971) is a brilliant indication of what can be achieved by such a feed-back.